FOREX
TRADING USING
INTERMARKET
ANALYSIS

FOREX TRADING USING INTERMARKET ANALYSIS

DISCOVERING HIDDEN MARKET RELATIONSHIPS THAT PROVIDE EARLY CLUES FOR PRICE DIRECTION

LOUIS B. MENDELSOHN
FOREWORD BY DARRELL R. JOBMAN

MARKETPLACE BOOKS®
COLUMBIA, MARYLAND

TRA
SEC

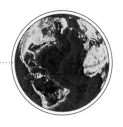

ISBN 1-59280-295-8

Printed in the United States of America.
    3   4   5   6   7   8   9   10

CONTENTS

Chapter 1
WHAT IS FOREX?   1

If you have traveled internationally, you may already know something about the forex market, today's hottest marketplace. Discover why you might want to trade forex.

Chapter 2
THE FOREX MARKETPLACE   11

The forex market is the world's largest marketplace, dwarfing all other markets combined. See how forex grew so large and how you can participate.

Chapter 3
FUNDAMENTALS AND FOREX   21

Forex traders can get plenty of information, sometimes so much that it can be hard to sift through it all. Here are some reports a forex trader needs to consider.

Chapter 4
APPLYING TECHNICAL ANALYSIS TO FOREX   35

With fundamental information overwhelming, many forex traders analyze price action in charts. Chart patterns and indicators have shortcomings, but see how predictive moving averages can help with market forecasting.

FOREWORD

IN THE EARLY 1980s, as the editor-in-chief of *Commodities* magazine, I was privy to a number of different trading ideas and techniques—so many, in fact, it was difficult to determine which was best or sometimes which had merit. This was during the heyday of innovations in the futures markets with the introduction of the cash-settlement concept in eurodollar futures, futures on broad-based stock indexes, crude oil futures, the pilot program for options on futures, and a number of other new contracts in areas where futures and options did not exist before. It also was the period when the personal computer was introduced and trading software was a new market analysis tool.

Inevitably, the developments in futures trading and in computerized market analysis using trading software began to come together, and it became obvious that the magazine needed to devote a lot more space to this subject. The problem was finding authors with actual trading experience who could explain the value of using this new computer technology for market analysis to readers without an academic background in computer science.

In early 1983 I received an article from Lou Mendelsohn. Lou and I did not know each other. He had a message about trading software that he was willing to share, and he knew that *Commodities* was the best way to reach a broad audience of futures traders. I just happened to be looking for good articles on that subject. What Lou submitted contained solid information on this new technology, and as a bonus, his article was well written. No one on the magazine's staff could have written such an article at that point because no one had the trading experience nor the knowledge of computers and trading software that Lou provided.

His first article entitled, "Picking Software Programs: Know Their Limitations," appeared in the May 1983 issue of *Commodities*. This article compared analysis software and system software in a logical, sensible way. At that time Lou recommended at least a 48-kilobyte computer—not the megabytes or gigabytes that are common today—evidence that this was a time when many traders were just learning how to use personal computers.

A second article, entitled "History Tester Important Factor in Software Selection," appeared in the July 1983 issue of *Commodities*. Lou emphasized the need for a history tester to compare the performance of different trading strategies and to have standardized performance reports so traders could make accurate comparisons of the results. Today we know about net return per trade, drawdowns, and all the other aspects of performance provided by software programs, but Lou's implementation of strategy back-testing in software for the personal computer was the first in the financial industry, long before TradeStation and other competing software programs appeared on the scene.

A third article, entitled "Execution Timing Critical Factor in System Performance," appeared in December 1983. By then, *Commodities* was called *Futures* as the move toward financial products had begun. In this article Lou analyzed the results of various entry and exit points in Treasury bill futures, one of the first articles featuring this type of research.

All of these articles illustrated Lou's thorough understanding of the markets and how traders could use their personal computers to analyze data and develop successful trading systems and strategies. This was new information to traders, and Lou's pioneering work was instrumental in incorporating the personal computer into the trading mainstream, particularly with the release in 1983 of his ProfitTaker software program. This was the first trading software program available for personal computers that performed strategy back-testing. ProfitTaker laid the foundation for much of the technical analysis software development that has evolved over the past twenty-five years.

Lou has continued to write extensively on the application of computer and software technologies to trading and has pursued various areas of research for the benefit of traders performing market analysis with their computers. Intuitively, traders know that a target market is influenced by developments in related markets and, in turn, the target market affects what happens in other markets. The difficulty is in quantifying those relationships. In the late 1980s Lou discovered that, by applying computerized "artificial intelligence" concepts, involving a mathematical technology known as neural networks, to market analysis he could ferret out intermarket patterns and connections between markets that could never be seen through chart analysis. He then used that information to forecast moving averages, making them a leading rather than a lagging technical indicator.

His research into intermarket relationships and predicted moving averages led to the development of VantagePoint Intermarket Analysis Software™, first released in 1991. The research has not ended there, however, as newly updated versions are released, all of which benefit from his ongoing research into the application of neural networks to intermarket analysis and incorporate new "learning" by the software through periodic retraining of the neural networks.

This book is a result of Lou's ongoing research, focusing specifically on the foreign exchange market, the largest trading market in the world. If there is a market that is perfectly matched to Lou's analytical approach of applying computerized trading software technology, such as neural networks, to intermarket analysis, it is the forex market because of the relationships of various currencies to each other and to other financial influences (i.e., interest rates, stock indexes in a global marketplace). As icing on the cake, forex is typically a trending market that makes it an excellent candidate for his forecasted moving average analysis.

As with those articles in *Commodities* and *Futures* nearly twenty-five years ago, this book presents sound, practical information about forex trading, focusing on the benefit of analytic trading software that can make highly accurate short-term forecasts of the market direction of this exciting and potentially highly lucrative trading arena.

DARRELL R. JOBMAN

Darrell Jobman is an acknowledged authority on the financial markets and has been writing about them for over 35 years. After spending nearly 20 years as editor of Futures Magazine Mr. Jobman is now Editor-in-Chief for www.TradingEducation.com. Mr. Jobman has authored and/or edited six books including *The Handbook of Technical Analysis* as well as trading materials for both the Chicago Mercantile Exchange and the Chicago Board of Trade.

PREFACE

THIS BOOK EXPLORES the application of intermarket analysis to the foreign exchange market, the world's largest and most widely traded financial market. Intermarket analysis helps traders identify and anticipate changes in trend direction and prices due to influences of other related markets as financial markets have become interconnected and interdependent in today's global economy.

These markets include forex futures and options as well as major cash forex pairs, which are affected not only by other currencies but by related markets such the S&P 500 Index, gold, crude oil, and interest rates. As the world economy of the twenty-first century continues to grow and as new advances in information technologies continue to be introduced, financial markets will become even more globalized and sophisticated than they are today, increasing the central role that the forex markets play in the global economy.

Since its introduction in the 1980s, intermarket analysis has become a critical facet of the overall field of technical analysis because it empowers individual traders to make more effective trading decisions based upon the linkages between related financial markets. By incorporating intermarket analysis into trading plans and strategies instead of limiting the scope of analysis to each individual market, traders can make these relationships and interconnections between markets work for instead of against them.

Forex markets are especially good candidates for intermarket analysis because of the key role of the U. S. dollar in most major currency pairs while other currencies tend to move in concert against the dollar. What influences one currency often influences many other currencies, usually not in lockstep but to a greater or lesser degree, depending on the circumstance. Knowing what is occurring in various currencies and other related markets can provide traders with both a broader perspective and greater insight into forex market dynamics. It can thereby provide an early warning of impending changes in trend direction in the target market. This allows traders to make more effective and decisive trading decisions than would be possible by relying on traditional single-market technical analysis indicators that too often lag the market.

This book is addressed primarily to traders and investors who use personal computers and the Internet to analyze forex markets and make their own trading decisions. The book also offers insights into how day traders and position traders in both the cash and futures markets can improve their trading performance and achieve a serious competitive advantage in today's globally interdependent financial markets. It will interest both experienced traders and newcomers to forex markets who are inclined toward technical analysis and recognize the potential financial benefits of incorporating intermarket analysis into their trading strategies.

Louis B. Mendelsohn

INTRODUCTION

I RECOUNTED HOW I GOT INVOLVED in commodity futures trading and computerized technical analysis in my 2000 book, *Trend Forecasting with Technical Analysis: Unleashing the Hidden Power of Intermarket Analysis to Beat the Market.* However, I believe that it is worth repeating the highlights here because they address the convergence of the development of futures trading and trading software technology during the 1980s and 1990s that is now applied in today's hot forex markets.

I traded stocks and options for nearly a decade, using various technical analysis methods before I began day trading and position trading commodities in the late 1970s while employed as a hospital administrator for Humana, one of the largest for-profit hospital management companies in the United States at that time. A physician friend who traded gold futures provided the encouragement that moved me from equities into this new trading area. This was during the inflationary period when gold prices were building to a peak above $800 an ounce, so there was incredible market excitement surrounding commodities trading.

At first I subscribed to weekly chart services, which had to be updated by hand during the week and required a very sharp pencil to draw my support and resistance lines, which in turn determined where I placed my stops. It was very annoying to anticipate the trend direction correctly, only to miss out on a big move after being stopped out prematurely at a loss due to an ill-placed stop.

With only a handheld calculator available to compute numbers in the years before microcomputers, I learned the underlying theories and mathematical equations for numerous technical indicators, such as moving averages, and devised mathematical shortcuts to expedite my daily calculations.

I was quite excited when I brought home my first personal computer in the late 1970s. Soon I was teaching myself programming and writing simple software programs to automate many of these calculations.

I quickly realized that the marriage of technical analysis with micro-computers would revolutionize financial market analysis and trad-ing. Although I had been hooked on financial markets and technical analysis for nearly a decade by then, it was the prospect of applying computing technology to technical analysis that crystallized the intel-lectual passion that I had long sought.

In 1979 at the age of 31 and intent on pursuing this goal, I started a trading software company that was the predecessor to my current com-pany, Market Technologies, LLC. A year later, with my wife Illyce's support and, more importantly, with her income, I left Humana to trade commodities full-time while continuing to develop trading software. My goal was to design technical analysis software that would do more than just speed up the analysis calculations that I had been doing by hand each evening with a calculator. I wanted to test and compare various trading strategies that I had created to identify the best ones and fore-cast the trend directions of the commodities markets that I traded.

Working alone and at a feverish pace, I spent day and night for the next few years focused intently on my daily trading activities, researching more about the commodities markets, studying books and articles on technical analysis, examining every one of my winning and losing trades for patterns to incorporate into my trading strategies, and devel-oping trading software for the microcomputers that were just becoming fashionable among commodities traders.

In 1983, after three years of full-time research and development in which I was basically operating as a one-man think tank, I released ProfitTaker Futures Trading software, which offered both automated strategy back-testing capabilities and optimization. It was hot! It even did back-testing on actual commodity contracts with a built-in "rollover" function that moved from an expiring contract into the next actively traded contract. This same year, I authored a series of articles on technical analysis software for *Commodities* magazine (now known as *Futures*) in which I introduced the concept of strategy back-testing and optimization for microcomputers and outlined the impact that this innovation would have on technical analysis and trading.

I was encouraged in those early years by several prominent technicians and traders. Foremost among them was Darrell Jobman at *Commodities* magazine. Had he not seen the potential of applying computer technology and trading software to the markets when this new technology was in its infancy and had he not supported these efforts by publishing articles on the subject in his magazine, there is no telling what route the application of computer software technology to technical analysis might have taken.

For the next few years, I continued my software development efforts with ProfitTaker, wrote many more articles, collaborated on books on trading, and spoke at trading conferences at which I warned about the dangers of curve-fitting and over-optimization. Now that strategy back-testing is an integral part of today's single-market technical analysis software, I actually find it somewhat amusing (whereas as recently as the late 1990s I often found it annoying) when I hear new traders, who are just learning the ABCs of technical analysis, say that strategy testing has *always* been in trading software—as if airplanes have *always* taken off and landed. Little do they realize how much effort it took to implement rollover back-testing on commodity contracts on an Apple II+ computer with just two floppy disk drives.

By the mid-1980s, through my observations of changes in how the markets interact, it had become apparent that the prevailing single-market approach to trading software was already becoming obsolete. I concluded that technical analysis that looked internally at only one market at a time, such as ProfitTaker did, would no longer be sufficient, even with its strategy testing and optimization features.

Changes that were starting to occur in the global financial markets due to advances in both computing and telecommunications technologies, coupled with the emerging "global economy," made multimarket analysis absolutely necessary.

I realized that the globalization of the world's financial markets would mean that the scope of technical analysis and its application through the use of trading software to the financial markets would need to change drastically. As a result, I embarked on my next maniacal mission, which would result in the development of intermarket analysis software.

In that pursuit, the scope of technical analysis had to expand to include not just a single-market analysis approach, where I had focused my attention previously, but also an analysis of how related markets actually affect each other and, more importantly, how this information can be applied by traders to their advantage. My goal was to examine the linkages between related global financial markets so that they could be quantified and used to forecast market trends and make more effective and timely trading decisions.

In 1986 I developed my second trading software program, which focused on these market interdependencies. The program, simply named "Trader," used a spreadsheet format to correlate the likely trend direction of a target market with those of related markets, as well as with expectations regarding fundamental economic indicators affecting the target market. This trading software program, albeit quite primitive by today's standards, was the first commercial program available to traders in the financial industry to implement intermarket analysis.

When the stock market crashed in October 1987, my convictions about the interdependencies of the world's equities, futures, and derivatives markets were starkly affirmed. By then, I was sure that technical analysis would have to broaden its scope to include intermarket analysis, as the forces that would bring about the globalization of the financial markets continued to gain strength.

Despite my early efforts at developing intermarket analysis software, I was not satisfied with the underlying mathematical approach that I had used to correlate intermarket data in the Trader program and felt compelled to continue my quest for a more robust mathematical tool. In the late 1980s fortuitously I began working with a mathematical tool known as neural networks, which is a form of "artificial intelligence." I remembered this vaguely from academic material I reviewed while an undergraduate at Carnegie Mellon University in Pittsburgh in the late 1960s. A professor there, Herbert A. Simon, was an early pioneer in the field of artificial intelligence and its application to decision-making under conditions of uncertainty. In neural networks I found the right tool for my job! Neural networks had the ability to quantify the intermarket relationships and hidden patterns between related markets that were increasingly responsible for price movements in the global financial markets of the late 1980s.

In 1991 after considerable research in applying neural networks to intermarket data, I introduced my third and latest trading software program, VantagePoint Intermarket Analysis Software. I chose that name because I felt that intermarket analysis gives traders a different vantage point on the markets than is possible looking at just one market at a time. VantagePoint uses neural networks to analyze price, volume, and open interest data on a specific target market and between that market and various other related markets. The software then makes short-term forecasts of the trend direction and high and low prices of the target market.

At this same time, other technicians, working independently, began to explore intermarket relationships, primarily from an intuitive and descriptive standpoint rather than the quantitative approach that I had taken. One of these analysts, John Murphy, who at the time was the technical analyst for CNBC, lent further credibility among traders to the newly emerging field of intermarket analysis.

Since the late 1980s, I have continued to refine my trading software based upon neural networks applied to intermarket analysis and have succeeded at creating effective trend-forecasting trading strategies built around forecasted moving averages. VantagePoint, which at first only made forecasts for thirty-year Treasury bonds in 1991 when it was first released, now tracks nearly seventy different global markets, including stock indices, exchange-traded funds, interest rates, energies, agricultural markets, softs, and, of course, foreign exchange spot and futures markets.

The focus of this book is on how to use intermarket analysis to forecast moving averages, making them a leading, rather than a lagging, technical indicator for the dynamic forex markets.

FOREX TRADING USING INTERMARKET ANALYSIS

WHAT IS FOREX?

If you have traveled internationally, you probably are well aware of the foreign exchange market, often called the forex or FX market. When you converted U.S. dollars into euros or yen or vice versa at a bank or currency exchange, you may have noticed big differences in the buying power of your currency, depending on when and where you you made the transactions. Although you may have noted the impact on your pocketbook, you may not have realized that you were also participating in the largest market in the world.

The forex market trades an estimated $1.5 to $2.5 trillion a day. No one really knows what the actual figure is because there is no central marketplace for keeping tabs on all of the forex transactions around the world. The forex market is massive, dwarfing the $30 billion a day traded at the New York Stock Exchange. In fact, forex trading exceeds the combined volume of all the major exchanges trading equities, futures, and other instruments around the globe.

Although professional traders implementing sophisticated strategies account for most of the trading in the huge forex market, participation by individual traders has grown tremendously in recent years with the proliferation of the Internet, enhancements in personal computers and trading software, the launch of dozens of cash forex firms taking advantage of online trading, and the globalization of markets in general. The introduction of the euro on January 1, 1999, and the weakness of the U.S. dollar after peaking in 2001 also contributed to the surge of interest in forex trading. Increased numbers of individual traders became aware of the role of forex in global markets with an eye toward profiting as currency trends unfolded.

More international trade, reduced government regulation, expansion of democracy worldwide, the increase in private ownership and free enterprise concepts, and a greater acceptance of free-market trading principles should keep the forex market at the forefront of traders' attention for many years to come.

LOCAL VALUES, INTERNATIONAL IMPACT

Every country has its own currency to facilitate its business and trade. The value of one currency as compared to another depends on the economic health of the nations involved as well as the perception of stability and confidence in the political climate in those countries. As conditions change, currency values fluctuate to reflect the new situation. These fluctuations create challenges for corporate financial officers and institutional fund managers but also provide opportunities for traders who want to speculate on impending changes in currency values.

Changes in currency valuations have a significant impact on governments, corporations, and financial institutions. Currency fluctuations, particularly when they are abrupt, affect the performance of bottom lines and the prices for many commodities and other markets. The forex market probably has a more pervasive influence on worldwide economic conditions than any other market, including crude oil.

By their very nature, currencies entail strong intermarket relationships. It is obvious that a currency cannot trade in isolation and that the mass psychology that drives changes in the value of one currency is bound to have an influence on what happens to other currencies as well as other related markets. Because government policies and economic developments that affect currency values tend to evolve over time, currencies are good trending markets.

The key to successful forex trading is understanding how these currency markets relate to each other and how patterns of past price action can be expected to occur in the future as markets respond to ongoing financial, political, and economic forces. However, these patterns and trends are elusive and may not be obvious from the examination of price charts. Nevertheless, traders need to spot these patterns and trends early, to get into what are potentially highly profitable trades and to avoid others.

Clearly, intermarket analysis tools that can help traders spot these recurring patterns and trends in their early stages can give traders a broad perspective and a competitive edge in today's fast-paced forex trading arena. It was this realization more than twenty years ago that led to my focus on intermarket analysis and the development of intermarket-based market forecasting tools that could discern likely short-term trend changes based on the pattern recognition capabilities of neural networks when applied properly to intermarket data. The forex market, by its very nature, is an ideal trading vehicle for the intermarket analysis and trend-forecasting approaches explained in this book.

WHY TRADE FOREX?

The first question you may have is, "Why trade forex? Is not forex something that interests only bankers and big money managers?" The advantages of trading forex are explained in detail in Chapter 2. The characteristics of forex trading are described in this chapter, which should convince traders to include forex in their trading portfolios.

CHARACTERISTICS OF FOREX TRADING

Diversification. We live in a world where terrorist attacks can occur at any time and place; where geopolitical tensions over nuclear power, oil, human rights, and many other issues threaten to disrupt normal trade and economic relationships; where U.S. companies are investing heavily in China and elsewhere to reduce their labor costs; and where China, in turn, is trying to invest in U.S. companies. Economic uncertainty seems to be a way of life. Traders cannot express their investment concerns about these issues, whether for protection or speculation, in any individual nation's stock or interest rate markets. Forex is the only instrument that incorporates all of these areas of potential concern and serves as a distinct asset class for speculators and investors.

Global Market. Markets such as equities or interest rates tend to be traded locally during the business day in their own time zone. For example, Japanese traders focus on Japanese stocks, European traders on European stocks, and U.S. traders on U.S. stocks. All of these traders certainly should be aware of what is happening elsewhere as the global integration of financial markets continues. However, an event in Japan that directly affects Japanese stocks may not have the same effect in Europe, and traders of European stocks may not pay as close attention to what happens in the Japanese or U.S. stock markets.

Forex, on the other hand, is an asset class that is truly a global investment reflecting every economic development on earth. Whatever has an influence on currencies in Japan has an effect on what happens to currencies in London or Chicago. It is clear that intermarket relationships among currencies are extremely important in today's world.

Twenty-four-hour Trading. Forex trading begins Monday morning in Sydney, Australia (Sunday afternoon in the United States) and moves around the globe as business days begin in financial centers from Tokyo to London to New York, ending with the close of trading Friday afternoon in New York. Anything that happens anywhere in the world at any time of day or night affects the forex market immediately. It is not necessary for an exchange to open before the effects can be seen. The forex market is always open for trading.

Electronic Trading. With the advances of technology, specifically, the Internet and online trading, and electronic trade-matching platforms, most forex trade executions are instantaneous, getting traders into and out of positions with the click of a mouse once they make a trading decision. All of the benefits of electronic trading and updates of positions and current status are available to today's forex trader.

Liquidity. With the size of the forex market, around-the-clock trading, and electronic trade execution, illiquidity is not much of an issue in most venues of forex trading. There is almost always someone to take the other side of a position a trader may want to establish, no matter when the order is placed. Forex bids and asks tend to be tight and slippage minimal.

Leverage. Forex markets provide some of the highest leverage of any investment vehicle. Traders may put up only a few hundred dollars to control a sizable position worth $100,000. As a result, a small move in a trader's favor can produce a big return on an investment. However, traders must remember that leverage works both ways. A small move that is against a position can eat up the money in traders' accounts quickly if they are not nimble traders who take quick action to cut losses. What leverage gives, it can also take away.

Plenty of Information. Governments issue dozens of reports every month that influence the forex market (see Chapter 3). Information is widely disseminated by the financial media. With advances in the Internet and financial news services, prices and economic data are delivered within moments of being released and are available to all forex traders throughout the world. If anything, there may be too much information for traders to sort through, which has its own negative consequences.

Simplicity. Traders do not have to watch or analyze the reports and price movements of hundreds of companies or mutual funds, trying to figure out which to buy or sell. With all of the fundamental information coming from many sources every day, traders can make trading life easier by concentrating on the forex market because they can easily limit themselves to monitoring movements of a half-dozen forex pairs. In addition, traders do not have to worry about going short or selling on a downtick as they do with equities because it is as easy to sell as it is to buy in the forex market.

Good Technical Market. Once traders understand the basics of technical analysis and how they can apply a software program to trading, they can extend that knowledge to all forex markets without having to learn and understand a whole new set of market factors. Because currencies are influenced by government policies and economic developments that usually stretch over long periods of time, forex markets have a reputation for being good trending markets. As a result, if traders keep an eye on economic conditions and charts as they evolve, they may find that forex market moves are easier to predict than are movements in other markets. A glance at a currency chart such as the Canadian dollar is enough to show clear long-term trends (Figure 1.1), which often have enough movement within them to satisfy the trader looking for short-term swing moves, as indicated by the bold-face bars in Figure 1.2.

Active Price Movement. Whether looking at price movements within a day or over a number of days, currencies tend to have trading ranges that are wide enough to produce attractive trading opportunities.

FIGURE 1.1.

CURRENCIES TEND TO HAVE GOOD LONG-TERM TRENDS. THE CANADIAN DOLLAR
CHART ILLUSTRATES THE TRENDING NATURE OF CURRENCIES.

SOURCE: VANTAGEPOINT INTERMARKET ANALYSIS SOFTWARE (WWW.TRADERTECH.COM)

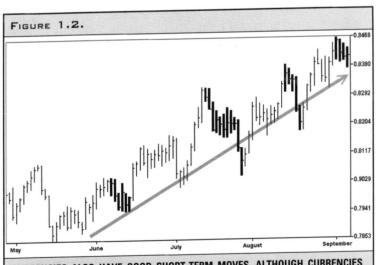

FIGURE 1.2.

CURRENCIES ALSO HAVE GOOD SHORT-TERM MOVES. ALTHOUGH CURRENCIES
OFTEN HAVE EXTENDED TRENDS, THE SAME CANADIAN DOLLAR CHART IN FIGURE
1.1 SHOWS THEY ALSO TEND TO HAVE TRADABLE COUNTER TRENDS THAT APPEAL
TO THE ACTIVE TRADER WHO MOVES INTO AND OUT OF POSITIONS.

SOURCE: VANTAGEPOINT INTERMARKET ANALYSIS SOFTWARE (WWW.TRADERTECH.COM)

Volatility is necessary for a trader to make money in any market, and the forex market usually provides more than enough volatility because there are new developments that affect the forex market every day.

Not Too Volatile. Forex markets can have abrupt price movements, but as a 24-hour market where price changes are always flowing through the system, forex markets rarely make the type of price move seen in stocks or futures. Stocks can plunge or soar 10 percent or more on some overnight earnings report or other announcement, leaving gaps on price charts when an exchange opens. A $3 change on a $30 stock is not that unusual, but a 10 percent move in a currency—for example, 12 cents if the euro were at $1.20—is quite unlikely.

In addition, while emerging markets may incur some extreme currency price movements, the major currencies are not like Enron, Worldcom, or dotcom stocks that fly all over the chart or even plummet and, like Refco, declare bankruptcy. If forex trading appears too volatile and risky, it may be a pleasant surprise for traders to learn that the forex market is probably more stable than the equities markets.

PAIRS, PIPS AND POINTS

Forex trading involves the simultaneous buying of one currency and the selling of another. Unlike markets such as soybeans or Treasury notes where traders are either long or short the market when they enter an outright position, forex traders are always trading pairs of currencies—that is, they are always long one currency and short another.

Forex trades are expressed in terms of the first currency of the pair. For example, a U.S. dollar/Japanese yen position—USD/JPY to the forex trader—means you are long the dollar and short the yen, believing the value of dollar will gain relative to the value of the yen.

The U.S. dollar is the key currency in many of these pairs. Together with the U.S. dollar, six other major currencies account for more than 90 percent of all forex transactions. These are the Japanese yen, euro, British pound, Swiss franc, Canadian dollar, and Australian dollar. The Mexican peso, Thailand baht, and dozens of other currencies are also traded in the forex market, and some have periods of active trading caused by extraordinary circumstances. For the most part, however, the forex trader can concentrate on just six major currency pairs that have the most liquidity:

- Euro/U.S. dollar (EUR/USD)

- U.S. dollar/Japanese yen (USD/JPY)

- British pound/U.S. dollar (GBP/USD)

- U.S. dollar/Swiss franc (USD/CHF)

- U.S. dollar/Canadian dollar (USD/CAD)

- U.S. dollar/Australian dollar (USD/AUD)

When currencies other than the U.S. dollar are traded against each other—for example, the Japanese yen against the euro (JPY/EUR)—these positions are known as cross-rates.

The first currency of a pair is the base currency; this is the main unit that traders buy or sell. The second currency is the secondary or counter currency against which they trade the base currency. The base currency has a value of 1.0, and the second currency is quoted as the number of units against the base currency. In the EUR/USD pair, you are looking at the number of dollars per one euro, the base currency—for example, 1.2000 dollars for each euro. In the USD/JPY pair, you are looking at the number of yen per dollar, the base currency—for example, 110 yen for each dollar—except in futures, which are covered in Chapter 2.

Changes in currency values are quoted in terms of "price interest points" or "pips." Pips are also called points and are similar to ticks in stocks or futures markets, the smallest increment of price movement. In most cases, a pip is a one-point change in the fourth digit to the right of the decimal—for example, a change from 1.1918 to 1.1919 for the euro. The value of a pip depends on the size of the contract or lot being traded, and that depends on where forex is traded (see Chapter 2).

THE FOREX MARKETPLACE

Although this book is about trading forex today and not about the fascinating history of currencies since the days of the Babylonians and Egyptians, it is helpful to have a little historical background to understand how and why today's currencies developed. The forex market is actually a relatively new development compared to marketplaces for equities, bonds, futures, and other financial instruments.

From the 1870s until World War I, gold backing provided stability for many of the world's currencies. Despite its long history as a store of value, however, gold was not without its shortcomings. When a country's economy was strong, it could afford to import more goods, which meant it sent more money overseas. A side effect of this was to reduce its supply of gold reserves to back its currency. With less gold to back its currency, money supplies had to be reduced, causing interest rates to rise, which then slowed economic activity until it brought about a recession.

The lower prices for goods during a recession eventually attracted buyers from overseas. The surge in exports increased the flow of money into the country, building up gold reserves and the money supply, reducing interest rates, and producing an economic expansion and sometimes a boom.

These boom-and-bust cycles were the norm during the gold standard days. World War I disrupted trade flow, and forex markets became very volatile and speculative after the war. The Depression of the 1930s and onset of World War II further disrupted normal economic and forex activity.

STRIVING FOR STABILITY

Governments, financial institutions, and the public all sought economic and forex stability as volatility and speculation became dirty words. In an attempt to design a new economic order for a postwar world, officials from the United States, Great Britain, and France met at Bretton Woods, New Hampshire, in 1944. With European economies and their currencies devastated by war, the United States became the world's economic engine, and the U.S. dollar emerged as the world's benchmark currency.

The Bretton Woods Accord established a plan to peg major currencies to the U.S. dollar and pegged the dollar to gold at a price of $35 an ounce. Major currencies were allowed to fluctuate in a band within 1 percent on either side of the standard set for the dollar, and no devaluations were allowed in an attempt to gain trade advantages. If a currency deviated too much, central banks had to step into the forex market to bring the currency back into its acceptable range.

These measures did provide the stability that helped the postwar recovery. However, as international trade expanded, the amount of U.S. dollars deposited overseas in the new eurodollar market mounted. Russia, for one, did not want to place its oil revenues in dollars in U.S. banks where they might be frozen by the U.S. government during the Cold War era.

With large amounts of U.S. dollars accumulating overseas that could lead to a massive demand for gold backing those dollars at any time, President Nixon announced in 1971 that the U.S. dollar would no longer be convertible to gold. That effectively meant the end of the Bretton Woods Accord, which was succeeded by the Smithsonian Agreement in December 1971, providing a wider band within which currencies would be allowed to fluctuate. Since countries have different resources, different economic growth rates, different political goals, and other unique circumstances, maintaining a float arrangement was doomed to failure, no matter what the size of the band.

With closer geographic and economic ties, European officials did not give up on the float concept. However, because they did not want their economies and currencies to be tied so closely to U.S. developments, they set up their own arrangement within which their currencies would float, which also did not last long. In 1978 these European nations then created the European Monetary System (EMS) to keep their currencies in alignment. That effort lasted until 1993 when the propped-up value of the British pound defended by the Bank of England failed to withstand the onslaught of speculators led by George Soros. Great Britain dropped out of the EMS, spelling the end of that attempt to control currency values.

The demise of the EMS opened the way for free-floating exchange rates by default because there was no structure in place to control currency fluctuations. Most currencies float freely today although the Argentine peso, Chinese yuan, and other currencies have been pegged to the U.S. dollar. The various contrived floating arrangements in Europe that lasted almost a half century finally gave way to the euro, launched on January 1, 1999. The euro got off to a shaky start but has become one of the main fixtures in the forex market as it trades freely against the U.S. dollar, Japanese yen, and other currencies. In fact, the euro has been mentioned often as a potential successor to the U.S. dollar as a benchmark currency.

FOREX TRADING MOTIVES

In this free-floating environment, forex trading volumes have increased remarkably in recent years as banks, other financial institutions, brokers, hedge funds, multinational corporations, individuals, and even central banks have become participants, often employing increasingly sophisticated trading strategies. There are three main reasons to get involved in the forex market:

- *To convert profits in foreign currencies into a domestic currency to bring gains back "home."* This applies primarily to international corporations that do business on a global basis and whose bottom line may depend to a great extent on how well they handle their forex transactions.

- *To hedge exposure to risk from changes in forex values.* If corporate treasurers are concerned about exchange rate risk between the time a deal is made, a product is delivered, and payment is made, they may want to lock in a profit with a forex position at a favorable rate rather than take the risk of losing money just because currency values might change. A U.S. pension fund may also hedge its exchange rate risk by using a currency overlay program traded by an outside money manager.

- *To speculate on changes in currency values.* Although there is a growing awareness of the usefulness of forex trading in commercial transactions in global markets, speculation is probably the primary reason for most forex trading today. There is no way to quantify how much of the forex trading volume is for speculation, but it has been estimated that more than 95 percent of all forex trading is for speculative purposes and has nothing to do with commercial transactions.

THREE MAIN VENUES OF FOREX TRADING

INTERBANK MARKET FOR THE BIG BOYS

The greatest share of forex trading takes place in the interbank market in the form of currency swaps, forwards, and other sophisticated transactions. The interbank market is a global over-the-counter network that includes, as its name suggests, the world's largest banks as its backbone along with other large financial institutions and corporations that have to be members of the network to participate.

There is no centralized marketplace in the interbank market, no standardized contracts, and no central regulator. Transactions are conducted between parties over the phone or electronically. Based on a call-around tradition, deals may involve billions of dollars as price, delivery, and other terms are negotiated, sometimes on behalf of customers but often for banks or institutions as they speculate on the price movement of currencies.

However, unless you are a corporate treasurer, a global money manager, or someone in a similar position, the interbank market is probably not something with which you will be involved. This is a complex market reserved for sophisticated, professional, and nimble traders. There are, however, places where traders have easy access to the same type of forex trading that the big boys have in the interbank market.

CASH FOREX TRADING

One of the fastest growing segments of trading in recent years has been in cash forex as dozens of new firms have sprouted up, taking advantage of online trading and less restrictive regulations. Controversy still surrounds the regulation of cash forex firms, and the National Futures Association and Commodity Futures Trading Commission have shut down a number of firms that they perceived to be "bucket shops" or perpetrators of fraud.

In fact, sometimes the biggest risk in cash forex trading is not the market risk from changing currency values but counter-party risk—that is, the risk that the cash forex firm will not perform its obligations and will deal unfairly with customers. Because traders' accounts depend on the creditworthiness and integrity of the cash forex firm with which they are dealing, evaluating a firm carefully is one of the first essential steps for the cash forex trader.

Nevertheless, cash forex trading offers a number of advantages provided traders are working with a reputable dealer and understand the risks of high leverage available at some of these firms.

Low Entry Cost. In some cases, traders can control a currency lot for only a few hundred dollars. A minimal account size of $5,000 is typical, but in many cases traders can open a cash forex account for less money than an account to trade forex futures, which have standardized contracts that are generally larger than the forex lots traded in the cash market.

High Leverage. Traders can control a $100,000 position at a cash forex firm with $1,000—that is, 100-to-1 leverage. Forex futures may require 5 to 8 percent of the value of a forex contract in margin as a performance bond, but cash forex requires as little as a 1 percent margin.

Guaranteed Limited Risk. The low initial requirements do not give traders much leeway for adverse price moves. However, many cash forex firms will take traders out of their open positions immediately when their equity falls below the required minimum amount.

Real-live Quotes to Trade. The cash forex firm provides traders with two-way bid and ask prices for a number of forex pairs via a free, streaming quote feed on a trading platform that usually also has some analytical capabilities, depending on the firm and the established arrangements. If traders click on the posted bid or ask price on the screen, the position is theirs at that price instantly. There is no slippage or a partial fill as may occur with forex futures where prices are changing constantly. Real-time quotes for forex futures usually require the payment of exchange fees, which can mount up.

No Commissions or Fees. Cash forex firms do not charge commissions, as such. With stocks or futures, traders may have to pay $3.95 or $9.95 or even $100 in commission rates for every trade. Cash forex firms do not make their money on commissions but on the difference in the bid/ask spread (the price at which they sell and the price at which they buy).

FOREX FUTURES TRADING

Although futures contracts generally came along somewhat later than well-entrenched cash markets, the opposite is true with forex futures. Chicago Mercantile Exchange (CME) introduced futures on currencies in May 1972, not long after President Nixon closed the gold window and before many currencies had achieved free-floating status. Forex futures have traded in a floor setting with trading limited to regular trading hours during the day for more than twenty-five years.

When CME launched its Globex electronic trading platform in 1992, electronic trading was limited to after-hours or overnight trading outside of the floor-trading hours. Then CME moved to side-by-side trading several years ago, allowing electronic trading almost around-the-clock, including during those hours when trading was taking place on the floor.

Volume has been booming since then to make CME's currency market the world's largest regulated marketplace for forex trading (Figure 2.1). In 2004 CME traded more than 50 million forex contracts, a 50 percent increase from the previous year, with two-thirds of those contracts

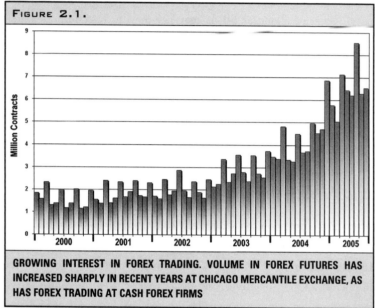

traded electronically. With CME making a major push to encourage trading in options on forex futures, forex volume is likely to get much larger at CME in the future.

FIGURE 2.1.

GROWING INTEREST IN FOREX TRADING. VOLUME IN FOREX FUTURES HAS INCREASED SHARPLY IN RECENT YEARS AT CHICAGO MERCANTILE EXCHANGE, AS HAS FOREX TRADING AT CASH FOREX FIRMS

SOURCE: CHICAGO MERCANTILE EXCHANGE

In addition to the major forex pairs and a dozen other currencies offered at CME, Eurex has moved into forex futures trading and the New York Board of Trade trades U.S. Dollar Index (USDX) futures. The USDX is not a currency, per se, but it does provide a good gauge of the value of the dollar against a basket of major currencies although trading in the USDX contract is not as active as trading in the major currency pairs.

Forex futures do have a few different quoting conventions than what traders will find in the interbank and cash forex markets. For example, the familiar quote for Japanese yen in the cash market is in the number of yen per dollar so traders will hear a USD/JPY quote of, say, 110 yen.

In the futures markets at CME, prices are quoted in the value of the currency as it relates to the U.S. dollar—for example, yen at 110 in the cash market would be 0.009091 in futures lingo (0.9 of a penny), often quoted as just 9091.

In addition to the benefits of cash forex trading mentioned earlier, futures exchanges provide some other advantages that may encourage trading forex futures.

One Central Market. Instead of having just one source providing bid/ask quotes as in cash forex trading—a source that incidentally knows your position—there are literally hundreds of traders, including major banks and financial institutions, making bids and offers all the time in futures. All of these bids and offers are channeled into one place, leading to the establishment of one price that is widely distributed the instant a trade takes place.

Tight Bid/Ask Spreads. With so many traders and so many bids and asks all coming into one location at one time, futures provide substantial liquidity and a smooth flow of trading from one price to another. The spread between bids and asks is small in forex futures, frequently only a pip or two, in a very competitive environment. Traders cannot count on that when they deal with only one firm facing no competition when it comes time to close out their position.

Transparent Pricing. The current price determined by these multiple sources is available to all traders of all sizes at the same time. Electronic futures trading does not play favorites but puts the small trader on an equal footing with the large trader on a level playing field. Traders are not limited to one set of bid/ask quotes offered by one firm and do not have to worry that prices may favor a dealer who may be factoring hidden spread costs into its quotes. All prices and all costs associated with forex futures trading are out in the open.

No Counter-party Risk. Traders do not trade with one firm and do not have to worry about the creditworthiness of the party that may be on the other side of the trade. In futures trading, the exchange's clearing organization is actually the counter-party to every trade, setting rules and policies to preserve the integrity of futures markets and provide a verified record of all trading activity that can be audited, if necessary. To date, no trader has ever lost money in futures due to counter-party default.

FUNDAMENTALS AND FOREX

The underlying cause of price movement in any market is fundamentals—those factors that affect the basic value of that market. For many markets, the focus is on supply and demand as free-market forces determine what is "expensive" or "cheap," depending on how much is available and how badly someone wants to buy or sell it.

Forex markets go far beyond basic supply and demand figures. Everything that affects the political and economic situation of the two nations involved in a forex pair has some bearing on the value of the two currencies against each other. Forex traders have plenty of fundamentals to consider as they are bombarded by news broadcasts, government reports, newsletters, brokerage firm research, television analysts, and many other sources.

In fact, the amount of information can be overwhelming. The challenge for the forex trader is not finding information but determining what is most significant from the enormous amount of information available and interpreting the likely effects on the markets.

Although it is more difficult to trade forex on the basis of fundamentals, forex traders do need to be aware of key fundamental factors, how they can move markets, and when they might have the biggest impact on markets. For example, traders may have a trading strategy that says they should buy the euro tomorrow, but tomorrow may also happen to be the day when a monthly U.S. employment report is scheduled to be released, or perhaps it is a day when the Federal Open Market Committee is scheduled to meet.

Such events can cause volatile market action that may influence how traders implement their trading strategy. Knowing about the possibility of potential adverse volatile movement as a result of some fundamental factor might, for instance, affect when to place a trade, what type of order to place, or whether to trade that day at all.

COPING WITH THE UNKNOWN

If a trader does not know something is going to happen, it is naturally pretty hard to prepare. How could a forex trader have prepared for the terrorist attacks of September 11, 2001, or for a massive tsunami, hurricane, or other natural disaster? Such shocks, though part of trading in the real world, fortunately are still infrequent. Even if traders could anticipate such events, they probably would not be able to predict how and to what extent the markets might react. The mass psychology of the marketplace sometimes does unexpected things. It is hard to trade unknown, untimed shocks.

If traders watch developments in markets and industries related to their target market, they may be able to predict that something is about to happen in the market. For example, if soybean traders had monitored ocean freight rates for the past month they might not be surprised if China announced an unexpected huge purchase that drives up soybean prices.

Sometimes traders have an inkling that some fundamental market-moving event is going to happen, but the timing surprises the market.

China's announcement in July 2005 that it would make a slight revaluation of the yuan and peg it to a basket of currencies instead of the U.S. dollar was just such an event. Discussed and expected for months, if not years, the timing still caught many traders by surprise.

Outbreaks of war, central bank interventions, government policy changes, trade embargoes, natural disasters such as hurricanes, announcements of disease epidemics such as Asian flu, and similar occurrences are events that traders expect will affect various markets. However, the timing or the extent of the action may catch traders off guard, causing at least temporary volatility or whipsaws that trigger undesirable market exposure or ill-timed entries and exits. Such occurrences are inherent in trading.

Traders may not be able to anticipate the fundamental market-moving events, but many of these shocks have only a short-term effect on forex markets. Politics and government policies usually evolve slowly and produce trends that are more likely to persist in forex than in many other markets.

PREPARING FOR THE KNOWN

While the timing of elections, meetings of the FMOC or European Central Bank, releases of government reports, and other such events are known in advance to traders, these events or announcements often produce market reactions that are not widely expected. However, these are situations for which traders can prepare with sound trading strategies that minimize the risk of being caught off guard. There are a few general points that should be made about these fundamental factors.

- *First, when a government releases an economic report, most of the numbers are estimates based on other estimates.* Yes, the estimates are tabulated by experienced officials who have access to extensive data, but they generally are not precise counts. Nevertheless, these are numbers that all traders have, and the market has to live with them.

- *Second, when traders react to the numbers or results, they may actually be responding to what the market expected rather than the numbers themselves.* A report that might seem bullish may instead send prices sharply lower. All traders know the market axiom, "Buy the rumor, sell the fact." In some cases, bullish numbers may not be bullish enough to drive the market higher, or bad news may not be as bad as expected, and prices actually go up instead. In addition to being aware of the date and time of a report or announcement, traders should also have an idea about what the market expects so they can reduce their chances of being surprised and hurt by subsequent price action.

- *Third, an outcome or number that may be bullish at one point in time may not be bullish at another time.* Perhaps traders have become conditioned to the contents of a report and do not react as expected. Old news is old news, and markets usually require something new to spark a price move.

- *Fourth, traders' analyses may be correct, but they may be too far ahead of what the market is "thinking," so traders may be positioned way before the market is ready to move.* The fundamental numbers may be just what they anticipated, but the timing of a price move is off because it takes time for traders to digest what they have seen.

U.S. WATCH LIST

As indicated above, many government reports and other actions have an impact on forex markets, some more directly than others. Listed below are some items that have the most effect on the U.S. dollar with a brief explanation of the significance of each. All of these items tend to have an effect on other items and markets so traders cannot look at one in isolation when they are performing their forex market analysis. Whatever approach traders use for forex trading, they should have an idea when these meetings or releases are scheduled because of the volatile but perhaps short-lived price moves that they may cause.

EVENTS AND REPORTS THAT AFFECT FOREX MARKETS

Federal Open Market Committee (FOMC) Meetings and Fed Actions. FOMC meetings take place eight times a year, spaced about six weeks apart. The FOMC consists of seven governors of the Federal Reserve Board and five Federal Reserve Bank presidents and determines the near-term direction of U.S. monetary policy. The Fed has several actions it can take to stimulate or tighten the U.S. economy to maintain a balance between too little growth and too much inflation, its major tool being the power to raise or lower short-term Fed funds interest rates. Almost as important as what the Fed does with interest rates is the statement it releases at the end of each meeting, suggesting the posture with which it views the economy and sometimes hinting at what it intends to do in the future.

The importance of interest rates cannot be overlooked by the forex trader. All else being equal, a nation with the higher interest rate will attract more money than the lower interest rate nation and will thereby have the stronger currency.

Beige Book. Each of the twelve Federal Reserve regional districts provides reports on the economic outlook for their region, and the Beige Book combines these reports into one composite view of the status of the U.S. economy. Information on economic conditions from this report often guides the FOMC in setting monetary policy. Reports from individual Fed banks, especially the Empire State Index from New York and the Philadelphia Fed report, may have their own impact on markets.

Index of Leading Economic Indicators (LEIs). Although most reports lag the market because they are based on past data, LEIs are a composite index of ten economic indicators that predict the health of the U.S. economy. Individual indicator readings may not provide much evidence of growth or weakness but can be helpful when combined with other indicator data.

Gross Domestic Product (GDP). This is the broadest measure of a nation's economic activity, providing the best overall indication of economic health. The U.S. GDP is released in three stages—preliminary, advanced, and revised. Any of these numbers can draw a reaction from traders in financial markets.

Balance of Payments. The monthly release of U.S. trade figures is a key day for forex traders. There are several aspects involved in the interaction between nations. The first involves the value of imports versus the value of exports in the monthly release of trade figures. The United States has been running a consistent trade deficit in recent years, and increases or decreases in that figure can move forex markets. Nations would naturally like to export more than they import, but the United States is in a crucial position as it is often regarded as the engine that drives world economies. Strong imports may be a sign of a booming U.S. economy and good news for those nations sending goods to the United States, but it may not be good for the value of the dollar.

The second important part of the interaction between nations involves current account flows, the amount of money flowing into a nation versus the amount of money flowing out. Large amounts of cash may flow into a country to buy stocks or Treasury instruments or other financial or physical purchases such as real estate. Cash has generally flowed into the United States and has been larger than the trade deficit, offsetting the negative aspects of that deficit on the dollar.

Employment Reports. The report with perhaps the biggest single impact on financial markets is the monthly report of U.S. non-farm payrolls released on the first Friday of each month. A key number in the report is the number of new jobs created. Generally, the more new jobs, the more money consumers can be expected to spend, propelling more robust economic growth. However, a number that is too big can raise concerns about high inflation rates and have ramifications on interest rates that affect the forex market outlook. Traders also analyze components of the report, such as the average hourly workweek and average hourly earnings.

Consumer Price Index (CPI) and Producer Price Index (PPI).

Mention inflation rates, and traders usually think of the CPI or PPI, which measure price levels of various goods and services against levels that existed during a base period. These reports are usually considered to be the best gauges of inflation. However, some analysts do not put a lot of credence in these numbers because they exclude prices for fuel or food, which may vacillate wildly due to weather or other circumstances and often comprise a large portion of consumer budgets.

Consumer Confidence. Consumer spending accounts for about two-thirds of the U.S. economy so what the consumer is thinking is vital information to forex traders because of the impact on many other economic reports. Consumer sentiment surveys are conducted regularly by the Conference Board, University of Michigan, and others to get a reading on consumer attitudes about the economic outlook.

Retail Sales. One area that may be affected directly by consumer sentiment is sales by retailers, especially at critical times of the year such as the Christmas holiday season. At these times, analysts pay particular attention to same-store sales for comparisons with previous years.

Housing Starts and New and Existing Home Sales. These reports provide another gauge of consumers' willingness to spend and the increasingly significant effect that housing has on the economy. People have to feel pretty comfortable and confident in their financial position to buy a home. More housing means more demand for raw materials such as lumber or copper and for appliances and all the other items needed to build and maintain a home. Sales of all those items affect economic growth and, in turn, the course of the U.S. dollar.

Durable Goods Orders. With increases in new housing and home sales comes the need to furnish those houses with refrigerators, washers, dryers, other appliances, carpets, couches, and other big-ticket items. Orders for these "durable goods" provide an indication of how busy factories will be and how much money they will have to feed into the economy.

Construction Spending. This report analyzes spending for office buildings, shopping malls, and other business purposes. As with the housing market and consumer confidence, the amount of building construction reflects how confident business owners are about the economy. They are likely to build new facilities or factories only if they think business will be good enough to justify expansion.

Institute of Supply Management (ISM) Index. This is one of the first reports each month that provides a composite index of national manufacturing conditions. Generally, analysts view index readings above 50% as an indication of an expanding factory sector and readings below 50% as a sign of a contracting manufacturing sector. Often, as manufacturing goes, so goes employment, which can have a major effect on other components of economic health. ISM reports are also available for various sectors and regions of the country, with the Chicago Purchasing Manager Index regarded as an early indicator of the national figure.

Industrial Production and Capacity Utilization. Industrial production measures the physical output of the nation's factories, mines, and utilities while capacity utilization estimates how much of factory capacity is actually being used. The manufacturing sector accounts for about a quarter of the U.S. economy. Factories would naturally like to maximize their usage, but if the rate of capacity utilization rises above 85 percent, analysts begin to worry that it could indicate an economy that is getting "over heated" and could lead to inflationary pressures.

Factory Orders. This report combines the dollar level of new orders for both durable and non-durable goods and also reflects the health of the manufacturing sector and, in turn, its effect on the job market and other areas.

Business Inventories. Once a factory produces goods, they have to be sold to businesses and consumers to produce profits. What is left on the shelves of manufacturers, wholesalers, and retailers is an indication of how strong or weak economic demand is and provides clues about the direction of factory production in the future.

Personal Income and Personal Spending. Comparing the estimated dollar amount of income received with the amount of dollars spent on durable and non-durable goods and services provides a good clue about whether consumers will be able to spend more or less in the future. If spending exceeds income, buying will naturally slow, perhaps leading to a downturn in the economy. If consumers have a surplus of income over spending, they will have money to buy more goods or bid up prices or put into investments such as stocks or savings accounts. Following the money trail is a good way to monitor a country's economic well-being.

INTERNATIONAL WATCH LIST

Because of the dominant role of the U.S. dollar in forex trading, the U.S. reports and events listed above tend to get much of the attention in the financial press. Forex traders also must keep an eye on developments in other nations with major currencies in the world's forex markets.

JAPAN

The Ministry of Finance (MoF) is probably the single most important political and monetary institution in Japan and, in fact, the world when it comes to guiding forex policy. It may take just a statement from a MoF official about the economy or the value of the yen to drive the forex market. Japan has been the most active country in using intervention or threats of intervention to protect against undesirable appreciation/depreciation of the yen.

The Bank of Japan (BoJ), Japan's central bank, has considerable independence for some aspects of monetary policy such as the overnight call rate for short-term interbank rates. The BoJ uses the call rate to signal monetary policy changes, which impact the currency. The BoJ also buys ten-year and twenty-year Japanese Government Bonds (JGBs) every month to inject liquidity into the monetary system. The yield on the benchmark ten-year JGB serves as a key indicator of long-term interest rates. The difference between ten-year JGB yields and those on U.S. ten-year Treasury notes is an important driver of the USD/JPY exchange rates.

Another Japanese government institution that has an impact on the forex market is the Ministry of International Trade and Industry (MITI). MITI looks after the interests of Japanese industry and defends the international trade competitiveness of Japanese corporations. It formerly played a bigger role than now in forex markets.

In addition to the normal stream of data (i.e., GDP, trade numbers) that affect most currencies, perhaps the most important economic report from Japan is the quarterly Tankan survey of business sentiment and expectations.

EUROPE

The single most important financial agency in Europe is the European Central Bank (ECB), which sets interest rates to maintain an economic growth rate of about 2 percent. In light of votes by several countries to reject a common constitution for the European Union, the authority and role of the ECB is not as clear as that of, say, the U.S. Federal Reserve.

Europe is comprised of a number of diverse economies and nations, which are still trying to work through the process of forming the European Union. A forex trader may be able to look at composite economic statistics for Europe but also has to keep in mind the numbers for Germany, France, Italy, and a number of other individual nations. What may help one nation could hurt another and vice versa.

Although the effect of some policies and decisions by European officials in Brussels may not be so clear, ECB actions in setting interest rates and determining other financial matters seem to be more accepted by financial traders. As a result, the euro has already become a major factor in the forex market although it was only launched on January 1, 1999. Even with its short history, the euro is considered by more countries as a possible reserve currency in place of, or in addition to, the U.S. dollar. It is one of the most actively traded currencies today.

ENGLAND

The Bank of England (BoE) is the central bank that sets monetary policy to achieve price stability for that nation, with an objective of maintaining the Treasury's inflation target at 2.5% of annual growth in the Retail Prices Index (RPI-X), excluding mortgages. The BoE has a monetary policy committee that makes decisions on the minimum lending rate (base interest rate), which it uses to send clear signals on monetary policy changes during the first week of every month. Changes in the base rate usually have a large impact on sterling.

The spread between the yield on ten-year government bonds, known as gilt-edged securities or just gilts, and the yield on the ten-year U.S. Treasury note usually impacts the exchange rate. The difference between futures contracts on three-month eurodollar and eurosterling deposits is an essential variable in determining GBP/USD expectations. The spread differential between gilts and German bunds is also important because of its effect on the EUR/GBP exchange rate, naturally the most important cross-rate because of the United Kingdom's close relationship with developments in Europe.

SWITZERLAND

The Swiss National Bank (SNB) sets monetary and exchange rate policy. The SNB sets its targets for the Swiss franc based on annual inflation rates. However, the Swiss franc is unique among currencies in that it is often considered a safe-haven investment in times of international turmoil and geopolitical tension. Forex traders may flock into the Swiss franc at the expense of other currencies as a way to ride temporarily through some international crisis, depending on traders' views about the seriousness of the situation.

The Swiss franc has historically enjoyed an advantageous role as a "safe" asset due to the SNB's independence in preserving monetary stability, secrecy of the nation's banking system, and the neutrality of Switzerland's political position, whether the world is at war or at peace. In addition, the SNB is known to have large gold reserves that contribute to the franc's solidity. Because of the proximity of the Swiss economy to the Eurozone (specifically Germany), the Swiss franc tends to be highly correlated with the euro, providing one of the most aligned currency pairs in the forex market.

HOW CAN TRADERS KEEP UP?

When you look back over the preceding list of fundamental factors—
the known and the unknown, the events and reports—you have to
conclude that forex traders trading on the basis of fundamentals have
an enormous amount of information to monitor and digest, especially
if they are involved in more than one or two forex markets. There is a
way that you can include all of these fundamentals in your trading by
observing just one thing: price, which is covered in Chapter 4.

APPLYING TECHNICAL ANALYSIS TO FOREX

Traders may find the long list of fundamentals that affect forex trading introduced in Chapter 3 somewhat daunting. That is why many traders tend to prefer technical analysis, a study of price action that can be applied to any market.

Technical analysis combines the influence of all the fundamentals affecting a market into one element, the current price. Rather than keeping up with all the fundamentals, traders can analyze price movements on a chart, knowing that the price synthesizes every factor known to the market at the present time—at least, in the perception of traders. Price is the visible reflection of all underlying market forces, much like limbs and branches are the visible parts of a tree while fundamentals are the roots that feed and nourish the tree's growth.

The information that forex traders really need for their technical analysis boils down to the answers to the following four questions:

- In which direction is the market heading?
- How strong will the move be?
- When will the current trend lose its strength, creating a top or a bottom?
- What will tomorrow's high/low trading range be?

Fundamental analysis alone cannot provide these answers, especially when traders are looking at only one market at a time.

In an effort to find the answers to these questions, new traders seem to follow the same path. After attempting to analyze and understand the fundamentals of a market, they realize that it is virtually impossible for individual traders to match their knowledge of the fundamentals with the professionals in the marketplace. Even for one market there are just too many fundamental factors with which to keep up in a timely manner.

STARTING WITH CHART ANALYSIS

Many traders start with basic chart analysis such as trendlines and chart patterns. Perhaps they were enticed by the if-you-bought-here-and-then-sold-there arrows in a promotional piece that showed them how they could become independently wealthy based on a hypothetical track record. Such tempting "pitches" may spur them into reading introductory books or magazine articles or viewing a video trading course. Much of the basic charting educational material today has not changed in more than thirty years except for the updated charts, graphs, and revised hypothetical track records.

Traders new to technical analysis are usually first advised to find the price trend. This is a particularly important tip for the forex trader as long-term trends tend to persist in currencies as compared to many other markets because government policies and economic developments usually do not change that dramatically overnight. So forex traders should always have in mind one of the technical analyst's favorite phrases, "The trend is your friend."

However, identifying the trend is not as easy as it sounds as a look at the chart of the Canadian dollar in Figure 4.1 illustrates. Looking back at the price action from the right side of the chart, the downtrend from

March until late May and the uptrend from mid-May to August seem rather obvious. However, viewing the chart from the left side as the price action unfolds daily, where would a trendline be placed? That is a subjective decision technical traders have to make.

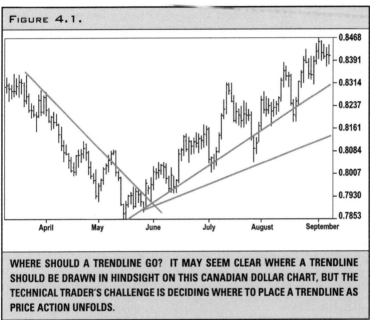

FIGURE 4.1.

WHERE SHOULD A TRENDLINE GO? IT MAY SEEM CLEAR WHERE A TRENDLINE SHOULD BE DRAWN IN HINDSIGHT ON THIS CANADIAN DOLLAR CHART, BUT THE TECHNICAL TRADER'S CHALLENGE IS DECIDING WHERE TO PLACE A TRENDLINE AS PRICE ACTION UNFOLDS.

SOURCE: VANTAGEPOINT INTERMARKET ANALYSIS SOFTWARE (WWW.TRADERTECH.COM)

If the trendline is placed too tightly along the tops or bottoms and trading decisions are based on penetrations of the trendline, traders are likely to be in and out of positions several times, which could prove costly. If the trendline is placed too far above or below the unfolding price action, this could also be harmful to a trader's account. In this case, a trendline along the initial lows in May, long before an uptrend was evident, would have meant the highs in July and August were well over three full points or $3,000 above the trendline. This means traders would have surrendered a large potential profit if they waited for prices to fall and penetrate the trendline to exit a long position.

ART, NOT SCIENCE

With such erratic up and down price movement, it usually does not take long for many traders to realize that chart analysis is a lot more art than science. This is evident with other chart patterns as well.

One popular chart formation that gets a lot of attention is the head-and-shoulders bottom or top (Figure 4.2). Traditional technical analysis says that a break of the neckline projects an additional move from the neckline equal to the distance from the top of the head to the neckline—in this case, roughly four points between the head and the neckline on the EUR/USD chart. Added to the neckline, the projected target is about 127. Is this really a head-and-shoulders bottom after prices kicked back below the neckline to test that breakout point? It is too early to jump to that conclusion on this chart. Meanwhile, the trader is left in a quandary about the market's prospects for becoming an uptrend.

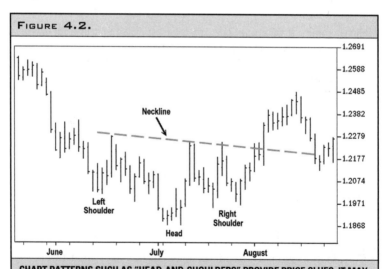

FIGURE 4.2.

CHART PATTERNS SUCH AS "HEAD-AND-SHOULDERS" PROVIDE PRICE CLUES. IT MAY BE A SUBJECTIVE OBSERVATION ON THIS EURO CHART, BUT THIS IS A HEAD-AND-SHOULDERS, A CHART FORMATION POPULAR IN TRADITIONAL TECHNICAL ANALYSIS THAT HELPS TRADERS SPOT BREAKOUT POINTS AND POTENTIAL PRICE TARGETS.

SOURCE: VANTAGEPOINT INTERMARKET ANALYSIS SOFTWARE (WWW.TRADERTECH.COM)

The USD/CHF pair in Figure 4.3 provides a few more examples of chart patterns. First is the flag, a brief correction in the uptrend that traditional analysis suggests is the halfway point of the move. At the time the flag occurs, that is not known, of course, but in this case that market axiom did turn out to be a correct assessment of the situation.

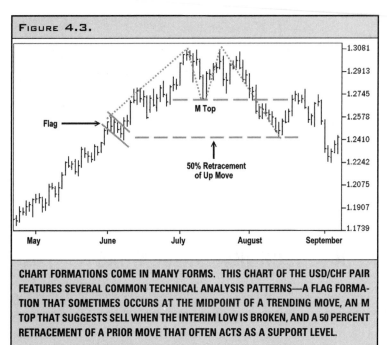

FIGURE 4.3.

Flag →

M Top

50% Retracement
of Up Move

May   June   July   August   September

1.3081
1.2913
1.2745
1.2578
1.2410
1.2242
1.2075
1.1907
1.1739

CHART FORMATIONS COME IN MANY FORMS. THIS CHART OF THE USD/CHF PAIR FEATURES SEVERAL COMMON TECHNICAL ANALYSIS PATTERNS—A FLAG FORMATION THAT SOMETIMES OCCURS AT THE MIDPOINT OF A TRENDING MOVE, AN M TOP THAT SUGGESTS SELL WHEN THE INTERIM LOW IS BROKEN, AND A 50 PERCENT RETRACEMENT OF A PRIOR MOVE THAT OFTEN ACTS AS A SUPPORT LEVEL.

SOURCE: VANTAGEPOINT INTERMARKET ANALYSIS SOFTWARE (WWW.TRADERTECH.COM)

The next pattern in Figure 4.3 is the double top or M top (turn the formation upside down, and you have a double bottom or W bottom). The market hits a high, backfills, and then makes a new run at that high, which proves to be tough resistance. With the M top, the second high is usually lower than the first high. When prices drop below the interim low, the top is confirmed, and a downtrend is expected. As with the head-and-shoulders pattern above, prices do not exactly cooperate, rallying back to the breakout line on this chart. Such is the fickle nature of chart patterns.

The third technical analysis point to note on Figure 4.3 is a 50% retracement of the upmove, which technical analysts traditionally see as a strong support area. In this case, it was. Prices bounced off that support on schedule, just as analysts who look for that type of retracement would have expected. It is one of several retracement areas that analysts project by using Fibonacci numbers and ratios.

Having prices perform as technical analysts expect them to is far from a sure thing. Spotting trendline breaks and top or bottom formations tends to be quite subjective, relying on the eye of the beholder. Chart signals usually are not as obvious as they might seem when you look at the price action with the benefit of hindsight. Even if you recognize a chart pattern, interpreting what it projects and then making a trading decisions based on that analysis are just as subjective. Because the chart pattern aspect of technical analysis is so subjective, back-testing is not really possible, so there is no way to measure the accuracy of this method of analysis.

ADDING TECHNICAL INDICATORS

Traders then typically start to look for something more quantitative on which to base their analysis. In looking beyond basic chart patterns, many traders turn to technical indicators, which may be able to detect changes in market momentum or strength or weakness that are not obvious when looking at a price chart. Many of today's analytical software packages usually include dozens of built-in indicators that are just a click of a mouse away so you do not have to do the calculations yourself or even comprehend how they were computed. Although these indicators can be back-tested and can be helpful in market analysis, they do share some general shortcomings:

- *First, most are based on only one thing: past prices.* As a result, they are all lagging indicators and not forward-looking indicators.

- *Second, using several indicators together may improve traders' perspective, but because they are looking at basically the same thing, adding more indicators does not necessarily result in better analysis.* In fact, it may lead to another technical analyst's catch phrase, "Paralysis by analysis," which may cause traders to "freeze" and actually make it harder to make a trading decision.

- *Third, it is easy to curve-fit or over-optimize the parameters of an indicator to the past price action.* When traders examine historical price data, they may adjust the parameters to find those that performed best in the past, only to discover that they do not work quite so well in actual trading.

- *Finally, no matter what traders may see in promotional material, no one indicator is the elusive Holy Grail for traders, because there just is no such thing as the Holy Grail.*

MOMENTUM OR TREND-FOLLOWING?

Technical indicators can be broken down into two broad categories:

- *Momentum oscillator types that attempt to spot market turns in the early stages and are typically based on a scale from 0 to 100.* These indicators include stochastics, %R, relative strength index, rate of change, and a number of others.

- *Trend-following types that attempt to detect the trend and the strength or weakness of the trend.* These indicators include moving averages, moving average convergence divergence (MACD), and directional movement index including the ADX indicator, which measures the trendiness of a market. Moving average crossovers can also be very useful in spotting market turns, as will be discussed later.

The momentum oscillators evaluate how current prices compare to previous prices and provide clues about overbought or oversold conditions that suggest a possible change in price direction. These indicators are most reliable in non-trending situations when prices are moving up and down. However, in trending situations, these indicators may give a buy or sell signal early in the move and then just remain stuck on that signal as long as the trend continues.

Look at the euro chart with the stochastics indicator as an example of this problem (Figure 4.4). A downside crossover of the two stochastics lines above a reading of 80 indicates sell, and an upside crossover

FIGURE 4.4.

INDICATORS PROVIDE MORE OBJECTIVE INFORMATION. INDICATORS SUCH AS STOCHASTICS CAN PROVIDE TIMELY SIGNALS IN CHOPPY MARKETS BUT BECOME UNRELIABLE WHEN MARKETS TREND, AS THIS EURO CHART ILLUSTRATES. THEIR BEST USE MAY BE IN SPOTTING DIVERGENCE—PRICES GO ONE WAY AND THE INDICATOR GOES ANOTHER.

SOURCE: VANTAGEPOINT INTERMARKET ANALYSIS SOFTWARE (WWW.TRADERTECH.COM)

below 20 indicates buy. Stochastics indicators give a good crossover sell signal at the high in April, but then show a crossover buy signal in May during the middle of the downtrend. After giving a signal too early, the buy signal provided by a stochastics reading below 20 persists for more than a month until the market finally does bottom in early July, making that indicator relatively worthless to the euro trader during the time the market was trending downward.

Even though the oscillator indicators often are not reliable in trending conditions, they can still provide some good clues about future price direction because of divergence—that is, while prices may hit a new high or low, the indicator reading does not. Divergence is a visible signal that the indicator is seeing some underlying weakness or strength not revealed by the price action. On the right side of the euro chart, note that the price rises to a new high, but the second stochastics high is lower than the previous high, a divergence from price action, suggesting the downtrend that followed. For these types of clues, forex traders may want to include some type of momentum oscillator in their analysis to confirm a signal provided by another indicator.

MOVING TO MOVING AVERAGES

Probably the most widely used indicator is some form of moving average. Moving averages are rather simple to understand and easy to calculate. Traders who do not want to do the math can just choose simple, weighted, or exponential moving averages from their analytical software. The length of moving averages can be adjusted quickly, depending on the trading time frame, and traders can use the closing price for a period or any combination of open/high/low/close.

A simple moving average is the sum of prices for number of days (N) divided by the number of days (N). As each new price is recorded, the oldest price is removed from the average and is replaced by the new price as markets move through time. Weighted and exponential moving averages are structured to give more weight to the newest price, based on the assumption that current price action is more significant to the near-term outlook than an old price that happened N periods ago.

Traditional technical analysis with moving averages is rather straight-forward. In the simplest arrangement, if prices move above the moving average, you buy and remain long while prices stay above the average; if prices fall below the moving average, you sell and stay short while prices remain below the average (Figure 4.5). Many traders use a combination of several moving averages, buying when the shorter average crosses above the longer average and selling when the shorter average drops below the longer average.

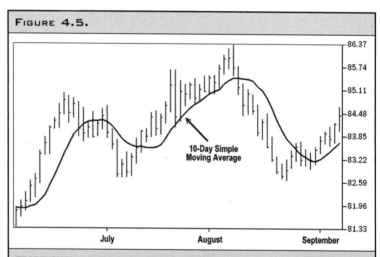

FIGURE 4.5.

10-Day Simple Moving Average

July   August   September

86.37
85.74
85.11
84.48
83.85
83.22
82.59
81.96
81.33

TRADITIONAL MOVING AVERAGES: A LAGGING INDICATOR. PERHAPS THE MOST POPULAR TECHNICAL INDICATOR IS A MOVING AVERAGE, SHOWN ON THIS JAPANESE YEN CHART. HOWEVER, BECAUSE IT IS BASED ON PAST PRICES, IT IS A LAGGING INDICATOR SUBJECT TO WHIPSAWS AND DOES NOT PROVIDE THE FORWARD VIEW A TRADER REALLY NEEDS.

SOURCE: VANTAGEPOINT INTERMARKET ANALYSIS SOFTWARE (WWW.TRADERTECH.COM)

Moving averages have the same problem as other indicators in relying on prices that have already occurred, meaning a moving average is another lagging indicator. Some analysts use displaced moving averages—that is, today's average is shifted several days into the future on a chart to reduce the lag effect of moving averages. Although this gives some semblance of a price forecast, it is a forecast based on past prices and prices that have not yet occurred, giving it a shaky foundation as a forecasting tool.

In addition, while the momentum oscillator indicators lose their value in trending market conditions, moving averages have the disadvantage of being subject to whipsaw moves when market conditions are choppy as prices vacillate above and below the moving average. Despite advances in technology and more sophisticated software, moving average analysis has remained much the same as it was years ago, and most traders still using traditional approaches to moving averages are no more profitable than ever before.

BROADENING THE MOVING AVERAGE VIEW

In order for traders to gain an edge by taking a position just as a price move begins to develop, they need indicators such as predicted moving averages that not only look back at past prices and patterns but also look forward to anticipate market action. In addition, they need tools that can look sideways at related markets to see how price action in those markets is affecting price action in the market that is being traded.

Weather forecasts for thirty days or ninety days into the future often are not that accurate, but forecasters have used technology in recent years to predict the weather accurately for tomorrow or the next few days. They forecast accurately the temperature highs and lows and the likelihood of storms or sunny weather. Their forecasts still are not perfect, of course, but the probability for the predicted conditions to occur has become quite high.

Most traders would be very happy to have a similarly reliable forecast for prices for the next two to four days. Using leading indicators that incorporate intermarket data, predicted moving averages can be calculated for the next few days. Forecasting future values of moving averages is easier than forecasting future prices themselves because moving averages smooth out the data and remove much of the market "noise" that clutters price forecasting. Through such financial forecasting, traders can develop mathematical probabilities and expectations of the future, which can give the traders a tremendous advantage over others still relying on single-market indicators that tend to lag the market.

For instance, VantagePoint software compares a predicted ten-day moving average for four days in the future with today's actual ten-day moving average as of today's close. It also compares a predicted five-day moving average for two days in the future with today's actual five-day moving average as of today's close. Then, if the predicted moving average is above the actual moving average, the trend is expected to be up and vice versa.

Figure 4.6 adds the predicted ten-day moving average to the chart in Figure 4.5 and shows how it compares with the actual ten-day moving average. Because the predicted moving average is being forecasted for four days in advance, note how closely it tracks market action and does not lag behind price turns as the actual ten-day moving average does. When the predicted ten-day moving average suggests that a top or bottom is forming before the actual ten-day moving average does or when the predicted average crosses the actual ten-day moving average, that is a signal to buy or sell because it means that the market is expected to make a turn.

BROADENING THE MARKET VIEW

Forex traders who want to tap the advantages of leading indicators such as predicted moving averages in today's fast-moving markets have to move beyond single-market analysis. It is still necessary to analyze each market to observe its chart patterns, trendlines, indicators, and so on because they are pieces of information that other trad-

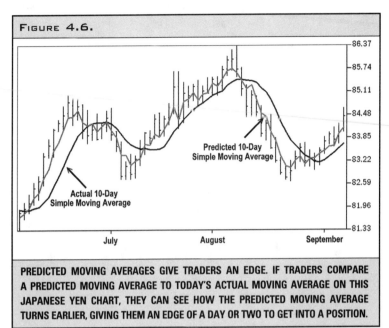

FIGURE 4.6.

Predicted 10-Day
Simple Moving Average

Actual 10-Day
Simple Moving Average

July   August   September

86.37
85.74
85.11
84.48
83.85
83.22
82.59
81.96
81.33

PREDICTED MOVING AVERAGES GIVE TRADERS AN EDGE. IF TRADERS COMPARE A PREDICTED MOVING AVERAGE TO TODAY'S ACTUAL MOVING AVERAGE ON THIS JAPANESE YEN CHART, THEY CAN SEE HOW THE PREDICTED MOVING AVERAGE TURNS EARLIER, GIVING THEM AN EDGE OF A DAY OR TWO TO GET INTO A POSITION.

SOURCE: VANTAGEPOINT INTERMARKET ANALYSIS SOFTWARE (WWW.TRADERTECH.COM)

ers are watching and using for their trading signals and can provide further insight about internal market dynamics.

However, with the influence of other currencies and other markets on forex in today's global marketplace, traders cannot afford to concentrate on analyzing just the internal market dynamics of one market at a time. Forex traders will have to pay more attention to linkages between related markets and the "market synergy" that drives these interconnected markets, as is explained in more detail in Chapter 5.

INTERMARKET ANALYSIS OF FOREX MARKETS

The previous chapters stressed the role of fundamental information and historical single-market price data in market analysis and the value of using these forms of analysis for the purpose of price and trend forecasting. As indicated earlier, traders must look at past price action to put current price action in perspective. However, in the real trading world, they must anticipate what will happen to prices if their analyses are to pay.

To look ahead with confidence, however, traders must look sideways to what is happening in related markets, which has a major influence on price action in a target market. What are the external market forces that affect the internal market dynamics of the target market—that is, the intermarket context or environment?

MOVING BEYOND SINGLE-MARKET ANALYSIS

Intuitively, traders know that markets are interrelated and that a development in one market is likely to have repercussions in other markets.

No market is isolated in today's global financial system. Single-market analysis, focusing on one chart at a time, has been traditionally emphasized. However, it fails to keep up with structural changes that have occurred in financial markets as the global economy has emerged with advances in telecommunications and increasing internationalization of business and commerce.

Many traders still rely on mass-marketed, single-market analysis tools and information sources that have been around since the 1970s. As a result, a large percentage of traders lose their trading capital. If traders continue to do what the masses do, is it not likely that they will end up losing their hard-earned money, too?

In the forex markets especially, traders cannot ignore the broader intermarket context affecting the market in which they are trading. Traders still need to analyze the behavior of individual markets to see the double tops, broken trendlines, or indicator crossovers that other traders are following because these are part of the mass psychology that drives price action. It is increasingly important that traders factor into their analysis the external intermarket forces that influence each market being traded.

HISTORICAL ROOTS

Intermarket analysis is certainly not a new development for traders, having roots in both the equities and commodities markets. Futures traders are probably familiar with equities traders who compare returns between small caps and big caps, one market sector versus another, a sector against a broad market index, one stock against another, and international stocks against domestic stocks. Portfolio managers talk about diversification as they try to achieve the best performance. Whether they are speculating for profits or arbitraging to take advantage of temporary price discrepancies, intermarket analysis in this sense has been part of equities trading for a long time.

Traders in the commodities markets have used intermarket analysis for a long time, trading spreads that have a reliable track record. Farmers have been involved in intermarket analysis for years although they may not have thought of what they do in those terms. When they calculate what to plant in fields where they have several crop choices—between corn and soybeans, for example—they typically consider current or anticipated prices of each crop, the size of the yield they can expect from each crop, and the cost of production in making their decision. They do not look at one market in isolation but know that what they decide for one crop will likely have a bearing on the price of the other, keeping the price ratio between the two crops somewhat in line on an historical basis.

The price relationships of corn to soybeans, hogs to cattle, gold to silver, or Treasury bonds to Treasury notes have been the subject of intra-commodity and inter-commodity spread analysis and have been an integral part of technical analysis of the commodities markets for decades, long before John Murphy and I brought the term "intermarket analysis" into vogue.

The commodities markets, in turn, have a tremendous effect on the financial markets such as Treasury notes and bonds, which have a powerful effect on the equities markets, which have an effect on the value of the U.S. dollar and forex markets, which has an effect on commodities. The ripple effect through all markets is a circular cause-and-effect dynamic, involving inflationary expectations, changes in interest rates, corporate earnings growth rates, stock prices, and forex fluctuations. You cannot name a market that is not affected by other markets or, in turn, does not affect other markets. Whatever the market, assets tend to migrate toward the one producing or promising the highest return. That is as true for forex as any other market.

Traders have probably heard the expression, "If the U.S. economy sneezes, the rest of the world catches cold" or that the health of the

U.S. economy is the engine that drives the global economy. It works both ways as a sneeze elsewhere in the world can have a significant impact on U.S. markets, as was evident during the Asian financial crisis in 1997 and other events over the years that have provided proof, if any was still needed, of how linked today's global markets are.

INTERMARKET ANALYSIS: THE NEXT LOGICAL STEP

A quantitative approach to implement intermarket analysis, which has been the basis of my research since the mid-1980s, is neither a radical departure from traditional single-market technical analysis nor an attempt to undermine it or replace it. Intermarket analysis, in my opinion, is just the next logical developmental stage in the evolution of technical analysis, given the global context of today's interdependent economies and financial markets.

The bottom line is if traders want to trade forex markets today, they have to use a trading tool or adopt an approach or trading strategy that incorporates intermarket analysis in one way or another. An important aspect of my ongoing research involves analyzing which markets have the most influence on each other and determining the degree of influence these markets have on one another.

Hurricaneomic Analysis[SM] is a perfect example of the interconnectedness of events and markets and how nothing can be viewed in isolation. Take the spate of hurricanes that hit the Gulf Coast and Florida in 2005. They did not simply cause local damage to the economy of those regions. On the contrary, there are hurricaneomic effects that will ripple throughout the world economy for months and years, impacting the energy markets, agricultural markets, building materials including lumber, the federal deficit, interest rates, and, of course, the forex market as it pertains to the U.S. dollar. So, hurricaneomic analysis goes hand-in-hand with intermarket analysis in looking at events such as natural disasters and their effects on the global financial markets.

Our research in the ongoing development of VantagePoint since its introduction in 1991 indicates that, if traders want to analyze the value of the euro against the U.S. dollar (EUR/USD), for instance, they not only have to look at euro data but also at the data for the other related markets to find hidden patterns and relationships that influence the EUR/USD relationship (Figure 5.1):

- Australian dollar/U.S. dollar (AUD/USD)
- Australian dollar/Japanese yen (AUD/JPY)
- British pound
- Euro/Canadian dollar (EUR/CAD)

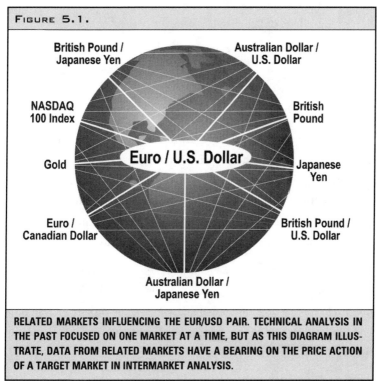

FIGURE 5.1.

British Pound / Japanese Yen

Australian Dollar / U.S. Dollar

NASDAQ 100 Index

British Pound

Gold

Euro / U.S. Dollar

Japanese Yen

Euro / Canadian Dollar

British Pound / U.S. Dollar

Australian Dollar / Japanese Yen

RELATED MARKETS INFLUENCING THE EUR/USD PAIR. TECHNICAL ANALYSIS IN THE PAST FOCUSED ON ONE MARKET AT A TIME, BUT AS THIS DIAGRAM ILLUS-TRATE, DATA FROM RELATED MARKETS HAVE A BEARING ON THE PRICE ACTION OF A TARGET MARKET IN INTERMARKET ANALYSIS.

SOURCE: MARKET TECHNOLOGIES, LLC (WWW.MARKETTECHNOLOGIES.COM)

- Gold
- Nasdaq 100 Index
- British pound/Japanese yen (GBP/JPY)
- British pound/U.S. dollar (GBP/USD)
- Japanese yen

When trading the USD/JPY forex pair, traders need to take into account another set of intermarket relationships including the following markets:

- Five-year U.S. Treasury notes
- Euro/Japanese yen (EUR/JPY)
- Gold
- Euro/Canadian dollar (EUR/CAD)
- Euro/U.S. dollar (EUR/USD)
- British pound/Swiss franc (GBP/CHF)
- Crude oil
- Nikkei 225 stock average
- S&P 500 Index

Many market interrelationships are obvious, but others may seem more distant and unrelated, such as the importance of stock indices, U.S. Treasury notes, or crude oil prices on pricing of the USD/JPY forex pair. Research has verified that these related markets do have an important influence on a target forex market and can provide early insights into the forex market's future price direction.

Additionally, through hurricaneomic analysis, data related to events such as the recent natural disasters in the U.S. can also be incorporated into forecasting models, along with single-market, intermarket, and fundamental data. This results in an analytic paradigm that I call Synergistic Market Analysis™ (see Chapter 8).

GOLD, OIL, AND FOREX

In some cases, the correlation is inverse, especially for markets such as gold or oil that are priced in U.S. dollars in international trade. The chart that compares the price of gold and the value of the U.S. dollar (Figure 5.2) shows that when the U.S. dollar declines, not only do foreign currencies rise but gold prices also rise. Studies on data from the last few years have shown a negative correlation between gold and the dollar of more than minus 0.90—that is, they almost never move in tandem but almost always move in opposite directions.

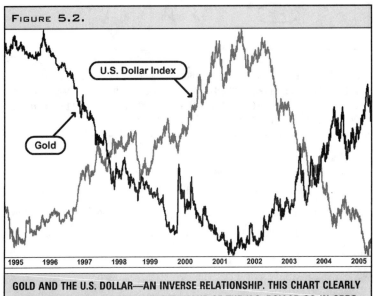

FIGURE 5.2.

U.S. Dollar Index

Gold

| 1995 | 1996 | 1997 | 1998 | 1999 | 2000 | 2001 | 2002 | 2003 | 2004 | 2005 |

GOLD AND THE U.S. DOLLAR—AN INVERSE RELATIONSHIP. THIS CHART CLEARLY SHOWS THAT GOLD PRICES AND THE VALUE OF THE U.S. DOLLAR GO IN OPPO-SITE DIRECTIONS MOST OF THE TIME, AN IMPORTANT INPUT IN INTERMARKET ANALYSIS.

SOURCE: VANTAGEPOINT INTERMARKET ANALYSIS SOFTWARE (WWW.TRADERTECH.COM)

The value of EUR/USD versus gold prices, on the other hand, shows a high positive correlation—that is, the value of the euro and gold prices often go hand-in-hand, suggesting these markets are both beneficiaries when funds are flowing away from the U.S. dollar (Figure 5.3).

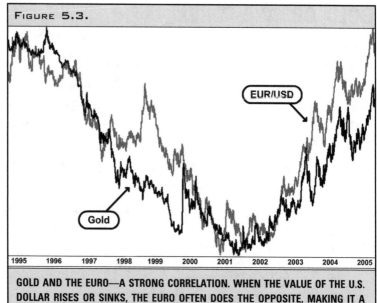

FIGURE 5.3.

1995 1996 1997 1998 1999 2000 2001 2002 2003 2004 2005

EUR/USD

Gold

GOLD AND THE EURO—A STRONG CORRELATION. WHEN THE VALUE OF THE U.S. DOLLAR RISES OR SINKS, THE EURO OFTEN DOES THE OPPOSITE, MAKING IT A GOOD MATCH WITH GOLD PRICES IF YOU ARE LOOKING FOR TWO MARKETS MOVING IN THE SAME DIRECTION.

SOURCE: VANTAGEPOINT INTERMARKET ANALYSIS SOFTWARE (WWW.TRADERTECH.COM)

Thus, gold prices are an important component in performing intermarket analysis of the forex market. If you see a trend or price signal on a gold chart, it may be a good clue for taking a position in the forex market, where a price move may not have occurred yet, or a forex move may tip off a gold move.

One of the factors cited for the rise in oil prices is the weakness of the dollar as foreign oil producers viewed increases in oil prices as a way to maintain their purchasing power in U.S. dollar terms (Figure 5.4). One way to counter the impact of higher oil prices is a weaker dollar, in what could become a vicious inflationary cycle.

Oil is a key commodity driving global economic growth, and oil prices and forex have a key relationship in the global economy. For example, when oil becomes expensive, it hurts the economy of Japan, which has to rely on imports for most of its energy needs. That weakens the yen. High oil prices benefit the economy of a country such as the United Kingdom, which produces oil, which strengthens the value of the British pound.

Because of the standing of oil in world business and commerce, anything that affects its supply or distribution is likely to produce a response in the forex market. This is why terrorist attacks or natural disasters such as hurricane Katrina, which threaten the normal flow of oil, often cause an immediate response in the forex market. A sudden shift from the dollar to the euro as the designated currency in crude oil contracts, as Mideast oil producers have mentioned from time to time, could also cause an immediate decline in the value of the U.S. dollar.

FIGURE 5.4.

U.S. Dollar Index

Light Crude Oil

1995　1996　1997　1998　1999　2000　2001　2002　2003　2004　2005

OIL AND THE U.S. DOLLAR—ANOTHER CRISSCROSSING CORRELATION. AS THE VALUE OF THE U.S. DOLLAR DECLINES, CRUDE OIL PRICES, LIKE GOLD, TEND TO GO UP AS OIL PRODUCERS TRY TO OVERCOME THE EFFECTS OF A FALLING DOLLAR. BECAUSE OF ITS CENTRAL ROLE IN GLOBAL ECONOMIES, OIL IS A KEY FACTOR IN INTERMARKET ANALYSIS OF FINANCIAL MARKETS.

SOURCE: VANTAGEPOINT INTERMARKET ANALYSIS SOFTWARE (WWW.TRADERTECH.COM)

Although these are the kinds of shocks that make market analysis difficult for any trader, the more typical scenario usually involves subtle movements taking place in intermarket relationships that hint a price change may be coming. If you are not using intermarket analysis, you probably are not going to pick up on all those relationships and the effects they have on markets, as those clues are hidden from obvious view.

Gold and oil are not the only commodities affected by changes in forex values. Exports of agricultural commodities account for a sizable share of U.S. farm income. When the value of the dollar rises, it tends to curtail buying interest from an importing nation as the commodity becomes too expensive in terms of that nation's domestic currency. When the value of the dollar declines, it reduces the price to an importing nation in terms of its currency and encourages it to buy more U.S. agricultural products. Instead of hedging their soybeans or corn, it may not be too far-fetched to suggest that U.S. farmers should be learning how to hedge the value of their production in the forex market.

Cotton is another commodity market strongly influenced by shifts in the forex market, especially with China as a major player in cotton because of its textile industry. Forex traders worried about the impact of China's revaluation of its currency on the world's forex market might even think about trading in the cotton market.

The influence that one market has on another market naturally shifts over time so these relationships are not static but should be the subject of ongoing study. Forex traders should also be aware that the impact from related markets may not be instantaneous. It may take time for a policy decision or other development to have an impact on the ever-changing marketplace. In addition, an influencing condition may influence a market direction for only a short period of time, so traders may have only a brief window in which to capitalize on a trading opportunity.

ANALYTICAL CHALLENGE

Intermarket analysis is not an easy task to accomplish for the average forex trader. The complexity of the dynamics between markets and their influences on each other mean that just comparing price charts of two currencies and producing a chart of the spread difference or a ratio between the two prices is not enough to get the full picture of a currency's strength or weakness or its potential for a price move.

Some analysts like to do correlation studies of two related markets, which measures the degree to which the prices of one market move in relation to the prices of the second market. Two markets are considered perfectly correlated if the price change of the second market can be forecasted precisely from the price change of the first market. A perfectly positive correlation occurs when both markets move in the same direction. A perfectly negative correlation occurs when the two markets move in opposite directions.

However, this approach has its limitations because it compares prices of only two currencies to one another and does not take into account the influence of other currencies or other markets on the target market. In the financial markets and especially the forex markets, a number of related markets need to be included in the analysis rather than assuming that there is a one-to-one cause-and-effect relationship between just two markets.

The correlation studies also do not take into account the leads and lags that may exist in economic activity or other factors affecting a forex market. Typically their calculations are based only on the values at the moment and may not consider the long-term consequences of central bank intervention or a policy change that takes some time to influence the markets.

The Canadian and Australian dollars, for example, are considered "commodity currencies." They may be highly correlated when a development influences raw commodity prices in general, and they may move in tandem as the value of the U.S. dollar or other major currencies move in the other direction by varying amounts. However, the Australian dollar is more sensitive to developments in Asia and may be more responsive to what is happening in that area of the world, at least for a while. Likewise, as China's currency becomes more significant in world currency markets, it may have more influence on the Japanese yen than on other major currencies. Developments in the British economy may keep the British pound from following the lead of the euro.

MULTIMARKET EFFECT

The forex market is a dynamic marketplace, constantly shifting and evolving. It is not one currency versus the world but all currencies affecting all other currencies to a greater or lesser degree. To attempt to examine the multiple effects of five or ten related markets such as forex simultaneously on a target market, reviewing five or ten years of data to find recurring, predictive patterns, methods such as linear correlation analysis and subjective chart analysis quickly reveal their limitations and inadequacies as trend and price-forecasting tools.

Single-market analysis tools cannot ferret out forex market interrelationships. If traders are serious about forex trading, they need to make the commitment to get the right tools from the beginning, or they are likely to struggle to keep their accounts intact. When it come to investing in analytical tools, another familiar saying: "Penny wise and pound foolish" is apropos.

Nothing, of course, is 100% correct, no matter what tools are used. Even the best tool can only provide mathematical probabilities, not certainties, but the tools do not need to be perfect to provide a trading edge.

If analytical tools can find and identify the recurring patterns within individual forex markets and between related global markets, that is all that is necessary to have a leg up on other traders. This insight into price activity over the next few days can provide added confidence and discipline to adhere to trading strategies and enable traders to pull the trigger at the right time without self-doubt or hesitation.

USING NEURAL NETWORKS TO ANALYZE FOREX

When all of the many shifting and changing intermarket relationships in the forex markets discussed in Chapter 5 are considered, traders might wonder how anyone could possibly pick out patterns and relationships from such a mass of data. The approach taken here to forecast moving averages is based on the use of neural networks applied to price, volume, and open interest data on each target market and various related markets.

Unlike the subjective approach of chart analysis, neural networks provide an objective way to identify and analyze the complex relationships that exist in forex and related markets. They reveal hidden patterns and correlations in these markets that cannot be spotted on a chart or through the use of traditional single-market indicators that tend to lag the markets.

A neural network is not a human brain, but it takes on some brain-like functions as it studies data, "learns" relationships within and between markets, recognizes patterns in past data, and uses this information to make forecasts about the target market. The neural net is essentially a modeling tool that accepts a variety of data and processes information in a manner similar to the brain (Figure 6.1).

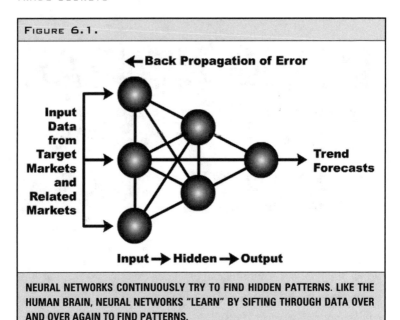

FIGURE 6.1.

←**Back Propagation of Error**

Input
Data
from
Target
Markets
and
Related
Markets

**Trend
Forecasts**

Input → Hidden → Output

NEURAL NETWORKS CONTINUOUSLY TRY TO FIND HIDDEN PATTERNS. LIKE THE HUMAN BRAIN, NEURAL NETWORKS "LEARN" BY SIFTING THROUGH DATA OVER AND OVER AGAIN TO FIND PATTERNS.

SOURCE: MARKET TECHNOLOGIES, LLC (WWW.MARKETTECHNOLOGIES.COM)

Neural nets were used in corporate decision-making, medical diagnostics, and many other applications before I began using them in financial forecasting in the late 1980s. Fortunately, traders using a program such as VantagePoint do not have to get under the hood and know exactly how neural networks function. Instead, they can concentrate on trading because expert developers have done extensive experimentation to develop the best trading model. However, to have confidence in a neural network trading model, it is worthwhile to have at least some understanding of neural networks and their training process.

INPUT LAYER

A critical first step in neural-network analysis is data input. The forecasts from a neural network are only as good as the data put into it. Collecting, cleaning, selecting, and preparing the data for analysis are all important. Neural networks are not limited to single-market data inputs nor are they limited solely to technical data inputs. The data goes far beyond just price or technical indicators, including volume and open interest for the target market, intermarket data from related markets, and even fundamental data.

With VantagePoint, for example, the raw data inputs involved in forecasting moving averages for euro forex futures include the daily open, high, low, close, volume and open interest for euro forex, plus the daily open, high, low, close, volume and open interest data for nine related markets.

Each VantagePoint program is designed specifically for a particular target market and uses five neural networks, in a two-level hierarchy, to forecast five different indicators for that market (Figure 6.2).

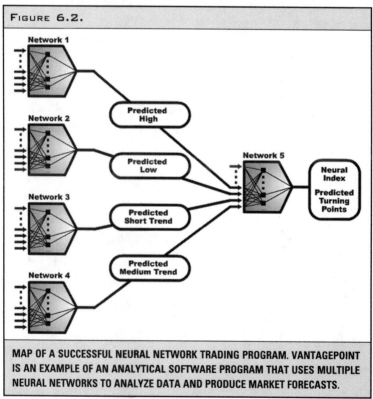

FIGURE 6.2.

MAP OF A SUCCESSFUL NEURAL NETWORK TRADING PROGRAM. VANTAGEPOINT IS AN EXAMPLE OF AN ANALYTICAL SOFTWARE PROGRAM THAT USES MULTIPLE NEURAL NETWORKS TO ANALYZE DATA AND PRODUCE MARKET FORECASTS.

SOURCE: MARKET TECHNOLOGIES, LLC (WWW.MARKETTECHNOLOGIES.COM)

- The first network forecasts tomorrow's high to help set stops for entry and exit points.

- The second network forecasts tomorrow's low to help set stops for entry and exit points.

- The third network forecasts a five-day moving average of closes two days into the future to indicate the expected short-term trend direction within the next two days.

- The fourth network forecasts a ten-day moving average of closes four days into the future to indicate the expected medium-term trend direction within the next four days.

- The fifth network indicates whether the market is expected to change trend direction within the next two days, by making a top or a bottom.

The first four networks at the primary level of the network hierarchy make independent market forecasts of the high, low, short-term trend and medium-term trend. These predictions are then used as inputs into the fifth network, along with other intermarket data inputs, at the secondary level of the network hierarchy, to predict market turning points.

Once raw input data have been selected, it is preprocessed or massaged using various algebraic and statistical methods of transformation, which help to facilitate "learning" by the neural network. That means it is converted into a form that the learning algorithm in the next layer can best exploit to get the most accurate forecasts in the shortest amount of time.

HIDDEN LAYER

The hidden layer is the learning algorithm used for internal processing to store the "intelligence" gained during the learning process.

There are a number of learning algorithms. The network recodes the input data into a form that captures hidden patterns and relationships in the data, allowing the network to come to general conclusions from previously learned facts and apply them to new inputs. As this learning continues, the network creates an internal mapping of the input data, discerning the underlying causal relationships that exist within the data. This is what allows the network to make highly accurate market forecasts.

Many different learning algorithms can be used to train a neural network in an attempt to minimize errors associated with the network's forecasts. Some are slow while others are unstable.

Training a neural network is somewhat like human learning: repetition, repetition, repetition. The neural network learns from repeated exposures to the input data, and learned information is stored by the network in the form of a weight matrix. Changes in the weights occur as the network "learns." Similar to the human learning process, neural networks learn behaviors or patterns by being exposed to repeated examples of them. Then the neural networks generalize through the learning process to related but previously unseen behaviors or patterns. One popular network architecture for financial forecasting is known as a "feed-forward" network that trains through "back-propagation of error."

Although a neural network-based trading program can accommodate and analyze vast amounts of data, one thing a programmer must avoid is "over-training," which is analogous to "curve-fitting" or "over-optimization" in testing rule-based trading strategies. It takes considerable experimentation to determine the optimum number of neurons in the hidden layer and the number of hidden layers in a neural network.

If the hidden layer has too few neurons, it cannot map outputs from inputs correctly. If a network is presented with too many hidden layer neurons, it memorizes the patterns in the training data without developing the ability to generalize to new data and discover the underlying patterns and relationships. An over-trained network performs well on the training data but poorly on out-of-sample test data and subsequently during real-time trading—just like an over-optimized rule-based system.

OUTPUT LAYER

The output layer is where the network's forecasts are made. During training, the network makes its forecasts, errors are computed and "connection weights" between neurons are adjusted prior to the next training iteration. Connection weights are altered by an algorithm—the "learning law," including the back-propagation method—to minimize output errors. Lots of adjustments may be necessary at any point along the way to get the desired results.

Two types of real number outputs in financial analysis include price forecasts, such as the next day's high and low, and forecasts of forward-shifted technical indicators, such as the five-day moving average value for two days in the future. The network developers have to decide not only what output to forecast but also how far into the future to make the forecast.

Then comes extensive testing to verify the accuracy of the network's forecasts. Testing is performed by creating an independent test file of data not used during the training process. In the testing mode the neural network is given these new inputs and uses the representation that it had previously learned to generate its forecasts so the network can be evaluated under real-time conditions. This is analogous to "walk-forward" or "out-of-sample" testing of rule-based trading strategies. The developers can compare performance results from various networks and decide which network to use in the final application.

As with other aspects of neural network and intermarket analysis research, there are a number of ways to evaluate performance of a neural network-based trading strategy. Traders should not attempt to tweak it by making human "adjustments" without going through the whole development cycle as such changes could undermine the accuracy and integrity of the network's forecasts and results. That is one reason why traders are not given the option within VantagePoint to make any change in parameters because the best parameter choices have already been defined after more exhaustive research than most traders could ever accomplish.

The result is a trading tool that is not only highly accurate but also very simple to use even by novice forex traders. Traders do not have to be rocket scientists to apply the forecasting capabilities of neural networks in trading the forex markets.

PROOF IS IN REAL TRADING

Obviously, no neural network nor any other trading tool can give you 100% predictive accuracy. Unforeseen events and random price action continue to produce uncertain markets. However, the most important focus is to achieve the most accurate market forecasts as possible. Neural networks are excellent mathematical tools for finding hidden patterns and relationships in seemingly disparate data and making highly accurate short-term market forecasts in a consistent, non-subjective, quantitative manner. This can be seen in test results with VantagePoint, which is nearly 80% accurate over all the markets it analyzes and forecasts (Figure 6.3).

If traders can appreciate the value of having intermarket-based trend forecasts, giving them a broader vantage point on the markets than could otherwise be achieved by focusing solely upon the internal dynamics of one market at a time, then traders will become believers in intermarket analysis and the power of neural networks as pattern recognition and forecasting tools.

FIGURE 6.3.

FOREX ACCURACIES

Australian Dollar / Japanese Yen	78.0%
Australian Dollar / U.S. Dollar	73.7%
British Pound / Japanese Yen	80.1%
British Pound / Swiss Franc	75.8%
British Pound / U.S. Dollar	77.2%
Euro / British Pound	72.6%
Euro / Canadian Dollar	76.7%
Euro / Japanese Yen	77.2%
Euro / Swiss Franc	73.6%
Euro / U.S. Dollar	72.2%
U.S. Dollar / Canadian Dollar	72.3%
U.S. Dollar / Japanese Yen	72.5%
U.S. Dollar / New Zealand Dollar	76.3%
U.S. Dollar / Swiss Franc	75.0%

VANTAGEPOINT ACCURACY FIGURES FOR EACH MARKET. NO METHOD CAN PREDICT MARKET MOVEMENTS WITH 100% ACCURACY, BUT VANTAGEPOINT'S NEARLY 80% ACCURACY RATES FOR SHORT-TERM FORECASTS PUT PROBABILITIES ON THE TRADER'S SIDE AND IMPROVE THE ODDS OF TRADING SUCCESSFULLY.

SOURCE: MARKET TECHNOLOGIES, LLC (WWW.MARKETTECHNOLOGIES.COM)

TECHNICAL TACTICS FOR TRADING FOREX

Once you understand the basics of trading in the forex market, know some of the fundamental factors that affect it and are familiar with various technical analysis approaches briefly discussed earlier in this book, including different technical indicators that help identify trend and momentum, the next big step is to move from theory to practice.

It may seem like this should be an easy process, but the fact is that it isn't for many, if not most, novice traders. Putting all of the pieces together about how the financial markets function and learning the nuances of trading, as well as formulating a coherent and sound trading strategy, can be an insurmountable challenge for new traders. Let's face it. If it were really as easy as some would suggest, every new trader would become a self-made millionaire overnight. But that's not the case.

FLOW LIKE A RIVER

So, your first practical task is to develop your own personal mindset for trading with which you can be comfortable. Fortunately for forex traders, this might come a little bit easier than for other traders because forex traders may already be more familiar with speculating on fluctuations in currency values.

Then you have to decide what sort of trader you want to be. There are trend-followers, contrarians, day traders, position traders, buy-and-hold investors, etc. Each approach has its own positives and negatives. Some may have more viability and appeal to you than others, depending on your risk propensity, available speculative capital, time constraints and financial goals.

Trading can be compared to floating down a flowing river, which twists and turns within its banks, sometimes quickly and sometimes more slowly. Floating along with the river's current is the easiest way to travel, because all you have to do is sit back and go with the flow. Admittedly, you can go against the flow, as many traders try to do in their trading, but doing so is much more difficult and frustrating and less likely to get you to where you want to go.

The problem is never the river. Its flow is never wrong since water always flows downhill. It's the same thing with trading forex or foreign currencies. The market is never wrong. The problem is always with the traders themselves who may try to fight the market's underlying current. When they find themselves in a losing trade, they are often unwilling to admit that they made a mistake or that this might not be the best trading strategy for them to continue to pursue. Too often, new traders wait until it's too late to adjust their course of action and end up becoming paralyzed soon after their winning position turns into a losing position that fails to turn around and quickly results in a large unnecessary loss.

Trading has also been compared to competitive sports. Every futures trade has a winner and a loser, since futures trading is a zero-sum game. What you need are analysis tools that will give you a competitive advantage to achieve your goal of making as large a profit as possible with the least amount of risk. Like a successful chess player, you should always be evaluating the ability of your opponents and looking ahead to your next moves if you want to be a successful trader.

As a forex trader, you should also develop an analytical routine, consistent with your own trading mindset that you apply whenever you are looking at the market and deciding about what trade to take. This process includes several basis steps:

F Fundamentals and the big picture. Based on your observations and fundamental information available to you, what is happening with the market overall? What are the events and issues that could influence currency values? Are prices rising, falling, or moving sideways?

O Orient current market action into the context of the big picture. Is the present market activity part of a larger trend or fluctuating within a trading range? Are interrelated markets moving in tandem? How are factors such as interest rates, commodity prices, or related financial markets influencing the forex market that you're trading?

R React. Once you have incorporated the market's current action within the broader context of trading and global economic forces, what are your conclusions about the course of action you should take? Your decision needs to be based upon actual facts as well as your trading mindset.

E
X Execute your trading decision by taking action to place orders based upon your understanding of the situation, including assessments of risk and the size of a position. This is the "plan-your-trade/trade-your-plan" axiom often cited by successful traders.

This FOREX process is not a one-time event for a trader but is instead a continuous loop of observations, orientations, actions, and reactions. In other words, every decision and every action generates new observations and reactions, which then produce new decisions and actions. The goal is to arrive at sound trading decisions and act more quickly than your trading opponents. Remember, the fact of life in trading is that someone is going to lose. You don't want it to be you.

Obviously, there are numerous technical analysis approaches, such as the trend and momentum indicators mentioned earlier in Chapter 4, which can be used in conjunction with each other in this FOREX process. One problem, though, is that most single-market indicators use the same underlying information—historical price data on just one market—to produce their trading signals.

Ideally, it would be more effective to use two or more indicators based on different data sets that have little or no correlation with one another. Volume and open interest, in conjunction with price, for instance, can provide a different look at market action. But volume and open interest seem to be less effective nowadays as confirming information in the financial markets including forex than they were in the past because hedge funds, money managers and other large traders appear to have altered the dynamics of trading in forex futures, especially near the end of quarterly contract expiration cycles, and there is no way to gauge volume in the cash forex market.

Volatility is another non-correlated input worthy of consideration for market analysis, but it can add even more complexity to a process that is already beyond the capabilities of most beginning traders and is, therefore, a subject that is perhaps best left to traders specializing in options.

So that leaves price as the major analytical focus. However, over-reliance on redundant indicators can lead to failure in today's fast-paced, global markets. That's why I have suggested that market indicators utilizing global intermarket data need to be incorporated into your trading strategies as part of the FOREX process.

To accomplish this, popular indicators such as moving averages, MACD, stochastics, and RSI, which look at trend and momentum and which are normally thought of as lagging in nature, can be transformed into true leading indicators using intermarket data as inputs into neural networks. Since the real underlying purpose of technical analysis from a practical standpoint is market forecasting, to the extent that leading indicators can be developed traders will have more effective tools at their disposal.

Additionally, other analysis tools such as candlesticks can be used in conjunction with various leading indicators to help you further confirm changes in trend and give you more confidence to take trades. I'd like to briefly discuss how candlesticks can be used in conjunction with forecasted moving averages to give you some more food for thought when you start to develop your own trading mindset and work through your FOREX trading process.

CANDLESTICK CHARTS ADD SPICE

Open-high-low-close bar charts provide the same information as candlesticks, but the latter does so in a much more visually appealing way. Compare the bar chart in Figure 7.1 with the candlestick chart in Figure 7.2. Both figures show the U.S. dollar/Canadian dollar cash spread for the same two-month period.

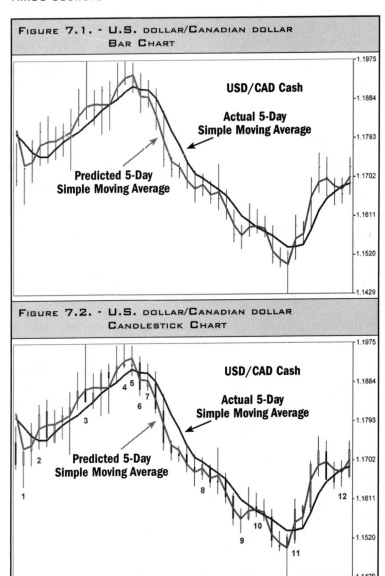

FIGURE 7.1. - U.S. DOLLAR/CANADIAN DOLLAR BAR CHART

USD/CAD Cash

Actual 5-Day
Simple Moving Average

Predicted 5-Day
Simple Moving Average

FIGURE 7.2. - U.S. DOLLAR/CANADIAN DOLLAR CANDLESTICK CHART

USD/CAD Cash

Actual 5-Day
Simple Moving Average

Predicted 5-Day
Simple Moving Average

BOTH CHARTS SHOW THE OPEN, HIGH, LOW, CLOSE PRICE INFORMATION, BUT
THE BAR CHART DOESN'T HAVE THE SAME VISUAL IMPACT AS THE CANDLESTICK
CHART, WHERE WHITE OR BLACK CANDLESTICKS HIGHLIGHT TRENDS AND PRICE
REVERSALS MORE CLEARLY.

SOURCE: VANTAGEPOINT INTERMARKET ANALYSIS SOFTWARE (WWW.TRADERTECH.COM)

The crossovers of the predicted 5-day moving average and the actual 5-day moving average based on closes are identical on both charts, but the candlestick chart depicts the strength or weakness of each day's price action more quickly at a glance. The long black or white candlesticks stand out, emphasizing the importance of that period's price action, and a series of black or white candlesticks illustrates the bearishness or bullishness of a trend more clearly.

Candlestick analysts have given various patterns clever names and have provided more descriptive characteristics for these patterns than is the case in typical bar chart analysis. Both types of charts have their double tops, inside days, gaps and other formations. But candlestick analysis ascribes more meaning to the candle "bodies" – price action between the open and close – and to the "shadows" or "tails" – price action that takes place outside of the open-close range for a period.

The chart in Figure 7.2 shows how candlesticks might be used to analyze price action in conjunction with other techniques such as predicted and actual moving averages. If you get a moving average crossover signal, it is instructive to see what that day's candlestick indicates. Or vice versa, if you see a particular candlestick pattern, it is worthwhile to know what the moving averages on that day suggest about future market activity. In this manner one signal can corroborate the other and thereby give you more confidence to act.

TWO MONTHS IN THE LIFE OF A CURRENCY SPREAD

Let's examine this chart in more detail.

1 – Hammer. After trending down, the price opens at about the previous close and then sinks. But the market rejects the down draft and closes higher, a bullish signal that the market has hammered in a bottom.

2 - Crossover signal day with bullish candlestick. When the predicted 5-day moving average crosses above the actual 5-day moving average, it does so on a day with a bullish candlestick, increasing chances of a valid buy signal. In this case, the market chops around for several days. Depending on your trading style, you may have been stopped out of the trade during this period although your moving average reading suggests sticking with a long position.

3 - Shooting star. The market shows some signs of weakness as it opens near the previous close, shoots to a new high and then falls sharply as traders reject the higher price level.

4 - Shooting star. After barely maintaining a long status (predicted moving average above the actual moving average), the market again makes another shooting star candlestick, reaching the previous high before being rejected again, warning that strength may be evaporating.

5 - Doji. Traders are a bit indecisive about which way to take the market as prices move up and down from the open during the day before settling at almost the same price as the open. A doji signal is a caution flag that adds weight to a pending top.

6 - Bearish engulfing pattern. The market opens higher than the previous close, then closes sharply lower with a long black candle body that engulfs the previous candle's body. The predicted moving average drops below the actual moving average on the same day. The strong negative candlestick reinforces the moving average crossover that signals a reversal to a bearish trend. A sell stop placed below the low of 6 would close out the previous long position and catch the new trend, if a downtrend materializes.

7 - Harami. The market isn't quite sure it wants to head down yet as price action on this day remains within the boundaries of the previous candlestick's price range – an inside day in

Western terms. It isn't until the following day that prices drop below the low of 6 and trigger the entry into a short position.

8 – Bullish engulfing pattern. After declining sharply for several days, the market hits a slight pause at 8 with the white body engulfing the previous candle body. However, the candle body is not very large and convincing. With the predicted moving average below the actual moving average, the trend indication is still bearish, and there is no reason to abandon the short position.

9 – Doji. Depending on how tightly you placed a buy stop, you might have been stopped out of the short position on the doji two candlesticks after 8 or after the doji candlestick at 9. But the moving average crossover signal is still in a bearish mode. A doji candlestick after a downtrend is not as reliable a reversal signal as a doji after an uptrend.

10 – Pause. A pause of several days takes the predicted moving average above the actual moving average, indicating a shift to a long position, but the action again to make such a switch is not very compelling. Buy stops placed above the candlesticks around 10 would not have been triggered, maintaining the short position as the predicted moving average once again slides below the actual moving average.

11 – Hammer and upsurge. The action between candlesticks 10 and 11 provides more conclusive evidence of a bottom as a doji is followed by a hammer – the market plunges to a low, then rejects the lower price level and rallies to near the high of the day at the close. The long white candlestick at 11 confirms the turn, and the crossover of the predicted moving average above the actual moving average suggests an uptrend. Again, it takes another day's action before the market is ready to move into its new trend.

12 – Pause. As often happens, the market reacts to the new trend by pausing – perhaps a flag in Western parlance – but the candlesticks do not provide any strong signal on direction. Stops placed below the lows would have maintained a long position at this point, but it would take additional bullish candlesticks to make the case for the uptrend to extend itself. You may need to make a quick adjustment in your thinking if the moving averages and candlesticks do not continue to support a long position.

TRADING A MORE CHOPPY MARKET

Although forex markets have a reputation for being good trending markets, they don't always trade in the longer, smooth trends shown in Figure 7.2. In fact, forex markets often make sharp, quick moves that make them a favorite of short-term traders but may be a source of consternation to traders who prefer longer-term positions but want to keep stops relatively tight to prevent a substantial loss.

As I said at the beginning of this chapter, how you trade will depend on your risk tolerance and personal trading style. In many cases, success isn't determined simply by taking moving average crossover and candlestick signals traded in a mechanical fashion, but has a lot to do with your whole personality, risk propensity and the extent of your trading experience.

The chart of British pound continuous futures in Figure 7.3 provides more of a challenge than the USD/CAD trending chart discussed above. Instead of the predicted and actual 5-day moving averages shown on the USD/CAD chart, the British pound chart shows predicted and actual 10-day moving averages, which provide a longer-term perspective but still catch trend reversals rather early.

The basic strategy described below involves trading a moving average crossover signal when it is corroborated by a candlestick signal, and placing entry and exit orders at points defined by typical traditional technical analysis techniques. You can use a number of strategies to trade this chart and may see other trades not mentioned.

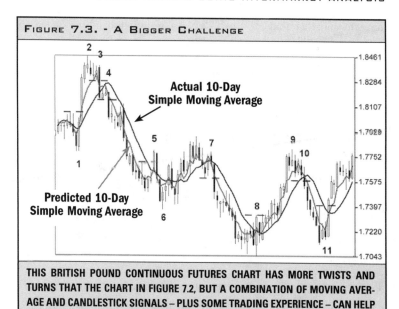

FIGURE 7.3. - A BIGGER CHALLENGE

THIS BRITISH POUND CONTINUOUS FUTURES CHART HAS MORE TWISTS AND TURNS THAT THE CHART IN FIGURE 7.2, BUT A COMBINATION OF MOVING AVERAGE AND CANDLESTICK SIGNALS – PLUS SOME TRADING EXPERIENCE – CAN HELP YOU TAKE PROFITS FROM MOST OF THESE MOVES.

SOURCE: VANTAGEPOINT INTERMARKET ANALYSIS SOFTWARE (WWW.TRADERTECH.COM)

1 – A tweezer bottom – two lows at the same level or a double bottom in Western terminology – and a long white candlestick that engulfs several previous candlestick bodies provides a pretty clear bullish signal to back up the signal provided by the predicted 10-day moving average crossing above the actual 10-day moving average. You could go long on the open or on a buy stop placed above the previous high (horizontal line).

2 – After several strong up days, a spinning top candlestick – small body in the middle of the day's range and shadows longer than the body – suggests the upmove may be weakening. The progressively smaller white bodies also make up a candlestick pattern called "deliberation", "advance block" or "ladder top." Whatever the pattern is called, it provides the first hint that the upward momentum is waning. A black candlestick that closes near its low and a doji further confirm a caution sign although at this point a traditional chart trader would also

have to consider that a bullish flag, a continuation formation, might be developing.

3 – Antsy traders might put in a sell stop below the lows to get out of a long position and protect profits (horizontal line). That stop would have been activated with the bearish engulfing candlestick. For traders looking for support for placing that stop or for going short, the predicted 5-day moving average did drop below the actual 5-day moving average on the day prior to the bearish black Candle 3 (not shown). As bearish as the situation might have looked, however, the predicted 10-day moving average has not dropped below the actual 10-day moving average to provide the longer-term position trader with a signal to go short yet.

4 – After a couple of small-range, inconclusive days, the predicted 10-day moving average does slip below the actual 10-day moving average, suggesting a short position. You could place a sell order below the low of Candlestick 3 (horizontal line) to get onboard the downtrend. The predicted 10-day moving average saw the reversal top about four days before the actual moving average made the turn lower.

5 – This choppy two-day pattern may irritate trend traders but is an inevitable fact of life in the real world of trading. Assuming you wanted to preserve profits after seeing some signs of a bottom provided by white candlesticks, you might have placed a buy stop just above the previous high (horizontal line) and would have been stopped out of your short position after a nice downhill run.

On the same day, however, the predicted 10-day moving average crossed above the actual 10-day moving average, a buy signal verified by a large bullish white candle. If you placed a buy stop above the Candlestick 5 high, the good news is that prices did not reach that level and you would not have gotten into a long position. The bad news is that the market immediately turned down again after taking you out of your short position and provided another moving average crossover sell signal for a short-lived decline.

6 – Another spinning top suggests the downmove is weakening, reaffirmed by several strong white candlesticks along with another moving average crossover buy signal. If you placed a buy stop above this high, as you did several candlesticks before, you would have gotten long just in time for another trip lower and another moving average crossover sell signal. That, in turn, reverted to another crossover buy signal on another strong white candlestick. In short, this choppy period would have been a challenge for your money management skills and is the type of situation where trading experience pays off.

7 – After this choppy period, the chart shows a moving average crossover to the downside in conjunction with a dark cloud cover candlestick – the market gaps higher on the open after a large white candlestick but then tumbles to close well into the white candlestick's body. This pattern needs confirmation from the following candlestick and got it the next day. You could have placed a sell stop below the dark cloud cover candlestick, getting you short on the open the next day. However, after the previous choppy period, you might have been a little leery about taking a signal and decided to wait for more proof of a downturn by placing your stop below a previous low (horizontal line). The timely signal provided by the predicted 10-day moving average crossover signal helped to capture another nice trending move.

8 – After running lower for about two weeks, the market produced a series of smaller-range candlesticks, indicating a decline in volatility. Many markets, including forex markets, tend to alternate between big candlesticks and small candlesticks or high volatility and low volatility. After a period of big candlesticks/high volatility, a market often shifts into a quieter consolidation period as it catches its breath with smaller

candlesticks/lower volatility. Conversely, after a smaller candlestick/ low volatility period, look for a breakout to larger candlesticks/high volatility, as neither type of price action continues indefinitely.

The key is determining which way the breakout will occur. If you put current market action into the context of overall market action – proximity to prior highs or lows, relationship to historical values, position in a trend, and other reference points – you should be able to get some clues about the likely breakout direction.

In this case, the smaller-range period included a hammer, doji and several spinning top candlesticks. All suggest some market uncertainty and indicate that the momentum from the previous trend is drying up. The moving average crossover to the upside and the big white bullish engulfing candlestick confirmed it. A couple of harami candlesticks (inside days to Westerners) followed as the uptrend signaled by the predicted 10-day moving average began to move out of its starting blocks. A logical point for a buy stop might have been above the high of the bullish engulfing candlestick, low enough to get an early entry into a longer-term uptrend if it developed but high enough to reduce the chances for getting caught in another choppy period.

9 – After a nice runup, including two big bullish white candles, the market starts to run out of steam. A shooting star – a candlestick that reaches a new high and then fades, leaving a long upper shadow – and several black candlesticks suggest the move might be over or at least weakening, a clue to tighten protective sell stops. In addition, for the trader keeping an eye on the bigger picture, the high at Candlestick 9 is approaching the previous high before Candlestick 7 several months earlier, which could become a resistance zone that may be difficult to penetrate.

10 – The predicted 10-day moving average turns down several days before the actual 10-day moving average and results in another mov-

ing average crossover sell signal on a bearish black candlestick. As before, a nervous, risk-adverse trader might have had a sell stop below the low of Candlestick 10 to protect profits.

However, for a new short position, it usually is not a good idea to anticipate a signal but is better to wait for the crossover signal to become evident before entering a trade. That means you may have to sacrifice some potential profit, assuming your signaled move develops, but it reduces the chances of being caught in a costly whipsaw trade if the new trend does not materialize. Of course, you can use the predicted 5-day moving average to get an earlier signal, or as you watch a potential turn shaping up, you may decide to enter a position near the end of the day if you expect that the close will result in a crossover signal on that day.

11 – A succession of black candlesticks turns a short position into a profitable trade quickly. In candlestick analysis, this pattern is known as eight or ten records down, but the criteria for the number of candlesticks varies. In this case, there are only seven black candlesticks, culminating in an interesting final candlestick bottom. On the final day of the downtrend, the market opens near the previous close, rallies above the highs of the two previous days and then collapses to close near the low of the day. At this point, the situation looked exceedingly bearish.

As I mentioned before, no market moves only in one direction or with such velocity forever. First, after an extended, rapid move like this, the market is probably oversold and due for at least a pause or bounce. Second, the slide took prices close to the lows established a month earlier, a strong support zone for starting a recovery in the opposite direction.

After a couple of harami candlesticks, the market had a breakout day to the upside with a big white bullish candlestick, reaffirmed by strong followup action over the next few days. A potential buy stop might have been placed above the high of the erratic last day of the downtrend (horizontal line) to protect profits from the short position. The moving average crossover signal to establish a new long position occurred a couple of days later, still in time to jump on the unfolding uptrend but with a caution sign as the market approached likely resistance from the previous highs.

NO MAGIC IN ANALYSIS

Remember, in every case you should be going with the market flow and not trying to force a position just because you have a moving average crossover and/or a bullish or bearish candlestick chart pattern. There is no one magic bullet or Holy Grail that will assure your trading success.

I have previously emphasized intermarket analysis using predicted moving averages because forex markets are especially influenced by intermarket relationships and because forecasted moving averages do exactly what an effective technical indicator is supposed to do: help you identify the onset of a trend in its beginning stages so you can get on board early and then tell you when to get out before there is a subsequent trend reversal. Beyond the effort to develop leading indicators that can provide more accurate market forecasting, I also recommend using multiple confirming indicators in conjunction with each other.

In a broader sense I believe that the next major frontier in the effort to expand the scope of market analysis will be to address the challenge of amalgamating single-market data, intermarket data, and fundamental data on global forex markets as well as futures markets into one coherent and quantitative framework that can be computerized and automated. I refer to this comprehensive analytic framework as Synergistic Market Analysis, which I will talk about a little bit more in the next chapter.

WAVE OF THE FUTURE: SYNERGISTIC MARKET ANALYSIS

When I began trading in the early 1970s, there were no stock indexes futures, no eurodollar futures, and no options on futures of any kind. Futures on currencies, gold, interest rates, energy, and options on stocks were all still in their infancy. There was no electronic trading and there were no personal computers to analyze the markets that I was actively trading.

The trading world has evolved considerably since then, offering many new markets to trade, especially in the financial arena; lots of different trading instruments; lots of trading software, and a global marketplace that features electronic trading around the clock. It is difficult to imagine that the next twenty-five years could offer as many trading innovations as those of the last twenty-five years.

Whatever the future holds, one of the most promising and lucrative trading areas is likely to be the forex market, which is so responsive to global economic shifts and geopolitical tensions. Years ago the forex market was limited to banks and financial institutions; individual traders were not part of the picture. Then came the trading prowess of George Soros and other currency speculators who were credited with bringing down the British pound in 1993, the Asian financial crisis in 1997, the launch of the euro in 1999, and other events that brought increased attention to the forex markets, both for speculation and as a means for knowledgeable traders to protect or hedge themselves against adverse changes in currency values.

The introduction of the Internet in the mid-1990s gave forex trading a big boost as it made it possible for individual traders to get information and to trade on a level playing field with any trader of any size any place in the world at almost any time of the day or night. As a result, numerous cash forex firms popped up in the late 1990s and early 2000s to accommodate this exploding interest in forex trading, making forex trading available to almost any pocketbook. Electronic forex trading volume has skyrocketed, and the growth in trading forex options promises to be just as dramatic in the next few years as exchanges facilitate that type of trading.

The global war on terrorism and other geopolitical, economic and hurricaneomic shocks and events will undoubtedly keep forex markets at the center of the global financial marketplace. The growing influence of China and other Asian markets on the global economy will affect many markets, the forex market foremost among them.

With unprecedented trading opportunities provided by the forex market, what the individual trader needs in today's world of speedy telecommunications and sophisticated trading techniques is what I call Synergistic Market Analysis, the synthesis of technical, intermarket and fundamental approaches.

INTERMARKET ANALYSIS

No country, no currency, no economy, and no market is isolated in today's global economy. Looking at one market means looking at a number of related markets to get the full story about the market forces driving any one market. With forex, that obviously means other currencies, but it also means interest rates, equities markets, and commodities, particularly international markets such as gold and oil. Single-market analysis just is not sufficient anymore.

ACCURATE, RELIABLE MARKET FORECASTING

The trader who wants to have an edge in today's trading environment needs to look ahead, using techniques and tools such as predicted moving averages that do not lag behind the market but have the ability to anticipate what is likely to happen to price and trend direction in the near future. Because of their trending tendencies, forex markets are especially good candidates for such market forecasting. Failure to incorporate leading indicators and information on related markets into trading strategies puts traders at a great disadvantage in competing with other more sophisticated traders, including professionals who make their livelihood trading forex markets.

Neural networks are not only well-suited to analyzing these markets from both a single-market and intermarket perspective but can also incorporate fundamental data as inputs. By using the computational modeling capabilities of neural networks in a structured framework that synthesizes these three approaches and integrates seemingly disparate technical, intermarket, and fundamental data, quantitative trend and market forecasting will continue to be at the cutting edge of financial market analysis in the early decades of the twenty-first century. Even hurricaneomic data can be incorporated into forecasting models. Literally any data that may have a bearing on financial markets can be used to determine its relevance to market forecasting.

TRADING EDUCATION

Many people get into trading with only a vague notion about how to analyze markets, how to trade them successfully, how to assess risk/return in trading, and many other factors that trading involves. With today's more volatile and erratic markets, education and information are even more important for successful trading in the future, and traders need to go to web sites such as www.TradingEducation.com for valuable assistance and free information on trading (see also the list of important web sites on page 97).

ADDITIONAL FACTORS AFFECTING SUCCESS

Even if traders take the Synergistic Market Analysis approach, myriad additional factors can affect their chances for trading success. These include mass psychology, judgment, trading experience, risk propensity, fear, greed, and amount of risk capital available. It is probably not possible to predict the trend direction of financial markets with more than perhaps 80% accuracy, due to randomness and unpredictable events, as well as the difficulty of developing effective forecasting tools. I am, nevertheless, determined to continue my research to push the forecast accuracy envelope as far as it will go; this has been my intellectual passion for the past several decades and continues to excite me. Fortunately, now, I am no longer a one-man research shop since forming the Predictive Technologies Group years ago, which is comprised of a team of analysts, researchers, and programmers, including Ph.D.s who can read books on neural networks as light bedtime reading.

I hope that this book will help traders become more aware of the implications that the globalization of the financial markets has on forex trading. By broadening their perspective to include intermarket analysis and various forecasting techniques that have been outlined in this book, I am confident that traders will be able to improve their trading performance by gaining more self-confidence to make better trading decisions, whether trading only the forex market or also trading equities, options, or futures.

TRADING
RESOURCE
GUIDE

SUGGESTED READING

THE VISUAL INVESTOR: HOW TO SPOT MARKET TRENDS
by John Murphy

It's technical analysis made easy! This bestseller shows how to track the ups and downs of stock prices by visually comparing charts - instead of relying on complex formulas and technical concepts. Includes software demo disks, step-by-step instructions for using charts & graphs, and more.

$55.00   ITEM #BC107x2379

INTERMARKET ANALYSIS: PROFITING FROM GLOBAL MARKET RELATIONSHIPS
by John Murphy

John Murphy on Intermarket Analysis updates the groundbreaking work of a well-known and highly respected technical analyst. A leading educator, Murphy walks the reader through his key tools to understanding global markets and shows investors where they can profit, bull or bear market.

$75.00   ITEM #BC107x1523697

TREND FORECASTING WITH TECHNICAL ANALYSIS: UNLEASHING THE HIDDEN POWER OF INTERMARKET ANALYSIS TO BEAT THE MARKET
by Louis Mendelsohn

Market methods from the last century won't work in this one and Louis Mendelsohn's breakthrough book takes technical analysis to a new level. Mendelsohn presents a comprehensive approach combining technical and intermarket analysis into one powerful framework for accurately forecasting trends.

$19.95   ITEM #BC107x11836

TECHNICAL ANALYSIS OF THE FINANCIAL MARKETS
by John Murphy

From how to read charts to understanding indicators and the crucial role of technical analysis in investing, you won't find a more thorough or up-to-date source. Revised and expanded for today's changing financial world, it applies to equities as well as the futures markets.

$80.00 ITEM #BC107x10239

TRADE YOUR WAY TO FINANCIAL FREEDOM
by Van K. Tharp

One of Schwager's famed "Market Wizards" answers the burning question: What's the one trading method that will bring you trading and financial success? A must read.

$29.95 ITEM #BC107x10245

THE ARMS INDEX
by Richard Arms, Jr.

Finally, it's updated and back in print! Get an in depth look at how volume - not time - governs market price changes. Describes the Arms' short-term trading index (TRIN), a measure of the relative strength of the volume in relation to advancing stocks against that of declines. A true trading gem.

$39.95 ITEM #BC107x3130

To order any item listed
Go to www.traderslibrary.com
or Call 1-800-272-2855 ext. BC107

IMPORTANT INTERNET SITES

Traders' Library Bookstore   www.traderslibrary.com

The #1 source for trading and investment books, videos, and related products.

Louis Mendelsohn   www.FutureForecasts.com

Includes information about Louis Mendelsohn, his personal library of articles, speeches, and book contributions, which are all available online.

Market Technologies, LLC   www.TraderTech.com

Includes extensive information on intermarket analysis, forecasting, VantagePoint, free sample forecasts, and much more.

Trading Education   www.TradingEducation.com

Educating traders in stocks, futures and forex markets. News, quotes, trading courses, software, and bookstore. Let Editor-in-Chief Darrell Jobman guide you to success.

Forex Trading Software   www.4xPairs.com

Trading software making predictions for thirteen forex pairs. Nearly 80 percent accuracy and free samples available at the site.

Chicago Board Options Exchange   www.cboe.com

Provides market data on indexes and stocks, quotes, charts, company reports, market commentary, and information on options trading.

Chicago Board of Trade   www.cbot.com

Provides news, market information, background on the exchange and various educational programs and seminars offered by the CBOT.

Chicago Mercantile Exchange   www.cme.com

Provides a wealth of information including price data, contract specifications, a news center, and background on the Merc.

New York Mercantile Exchange   www.nymex.com

Provides information on energy seminars and conferences, quotes, contract specifications.

New York Stock Exchange   www.nyse.com

Provides market quotes, a personal stock tracker and information on listed companies, IPOs, and equities trading.

Learn More About
VantagePoint Intermarket Analysis Software

▲ ▲ ▲ ▲ ▲ ▲

Discover how you can stack the odds in your favor when trading Forex by using VantagePoint Software—and its amazing forecasting capabilities . . .

It is no longer sufficient for traders to focus internally on single-markets in isolation of what related markets are doing. Intermarket analysis has become a critical ingredient to successful trading. To be competitive, traders must now have a broad intermarket perspective and the necessary analysis tools to implement it. VantagePoint Intermarket Analysis Software will give you a road-map—showing you what it expects the Forex markets to do—thereby giving you the self-confidence to take trades that should be taken—and keep you out of marginal trades that should be avoided.

VANTAGEPOINT:

- Forecasts all the major Futures, Commodities, Forex and ETF markets.
- Five neural networks make independent forecasts
- Reports offer detailed analysis on future and past forecasts
- Easy to read charts show you what's ahead

VantagePoint anticipates trends—it does not follow them!

VantagePoint was designed by experts who understand that to be successful in today's markets, you need to have a "heads up" on what is most likely to happen in each market tomorrow, not just what it has done today or in the past! Many traders are still use lagging indicators to make their trades, getting in and out of the market too late. VantagePoint uses leading indicators giving you a clear advantage.

VantagePoint Intermarket Analysis Software will place at your fingertips each evening:

- Predictions for up to 69 Futures, Forex and ETF Markets that are nearly 80% accurate
- Anticipated trend direction for the next 2-day and 4-day periods
- A projection of the next day's high & low
- The strength of the trend
- A heads-up on whether the market is expected to make a top or a bottom over the next 2 days

Plus . . . VantagePoint is quick and easy to use

- VantagePoint is ready to use when you receive it.
- You do NOT need to know anything about intermarket analysis or neural networks.
- You don't even need to know anything about programming. Unlike other complicated software programs, VantagePoint is easy to use and lets you focus on trading instead of getting distracted by the complexities of the software itself.
- The Daily Update function within VantagePoint automatically processes VantagePoint's five neural networks, which then generate their forecasts for the next day's trading. All you do is compare the Daily Reports (or charts) for several target markets to see which markets offer the best trades to take the next day. The process takes only a few minutes from start to finish.

What more do you need to be successful?

Discover the power of this amazing software program—and start stacking the odds in your favor today. Call us toll free for full details.

800-732-5407 (US & Canada) • **0-800-0186-502** (UK)
1 (800) 992-327 (Australia) • **1 (813) 973-0496** (International)
———————————— **Extension 100** ————————————
www.TraderTech.com/TLFX • email: **infoTLFX@tradertech.com**

MARKET TECHNOLOGIES
An Inc. 500 Company
World Leader in Market Forecasting™

Free 2 Week Trial Offer for U.S. Residents From Investor's Business Daily:

INVESTOR'S BUSINESS DAILY will provide you with the facts, figures, and objective news analysis you need to succeed.

Investor's Business Daily is formatted for a quick and concise read to help you make informed and profitable decisions.

To take advantage of this free 2 week trial offer,
e-mail us at customerservice@traderslibrary.com
or visit our website at www.traderslibrary.com where
you find other free offers as well.

You can also reach us by calling 1-800-272-2855
or fax us at 410-964-0027.

ABOUT THE AUTHOR
AND
MARKET TECHNOLOGIES, LLC

Louis B. Mendelsohn is President and Chief Executive Officer of Market Technologies, LLC and the developer of VantagePoint Intermarket Analysis Software.

Born in 1948 in Providence, Rhode Island, Mr. Mendelsohn received a B.S. degree in Administration and Management Science from Carnegie Mellon University's Tepper School of Business in 1969, a Master's degree from the State University of New York at Buffalo in 1973, and a M.B.A. degree with honors from Boston University in 1977.

Mr. Mendelsohn began trading equities in the early 1970s, followed by stock options. Then, in the late 1970s he started trading commodities, as both a day and position trader. In 1979 he formed Market Technologies to develop technical analysis trading software for the commodity futures markets.

In 1983, Mr. Mendelsohn pioneered the first commercial strategy back-testing and optimization trading software for microcomputers. By the mid-1980s strategy testing became the standard in microcomputer trading software for both equities and futures, fueling the growth of today's multi-million dollar technical analysis software industry.

Recognizing the emerging trend toward globalization of the world's financial markets, in 1986 Mr. Mendelsohn again broke new ground in technical analysis when he developed the first commercial intermarket analysis software in the financial industry for microcomputers. Building on his pioneering research in the 1980s involving intermarket analysis, in 1991 Mr. Mendelsohn introduced VantagePoint

Intermarket Analysis software, which makes short-term market forecasts based upon the pattern recognition capabilities of neural networks. Since then, Mr. Mendelsohn's research has continued to focus on intermarket analysis and market forecasting.

Mr. Mendelsohn has written extensively since 1983 in many prominent financial publications including *Barron's*, *Futures*, and *Stocks & Commodities*. He has been widely quoted in the financial media including the Wall Street Journal and Investor's Business Daily, has collaborated on more than half a dozen books on technical analysis, and has been interviewed live on national radio and television including CNNfn, Bloomberg Television, and CNBC. Mr. Mendelsohn's first book, *Trend Forecasting with Technical Analysis: Unleashing the Hidden Power of Intermarket Analysis to Beat the Market*, was released in December 2000.

Because of his achievements in the application of computers and information technologies to technical analysis over the past quarter century, Mr. Mendelsohn's biography is included in *Marquis Who's Who in the World, Who's Who in America, Who's Who in Finance and Industry*, and in a time capsule at the White House in Washington, D.C. He has been a full member of the Market Technicians Association since 1988 and a colleague of the International Federation of Technical Analysts.

Mr. Mendelsohn has also spoken at numerous financial conferences and symposia, including the Futures Industry Association annual meeting, Futures Symposium International, the Harvard Business School Alumni Club, Futures Truth, and the annual meeting of the Association for Investment Management and Research.

Since its founding by Mr. Mendelsohn, Market Technologies has been at the forefront of development of state-of-the-art technical analysis tools and information technologies for the financial markets. Located in the Tampa Bay area on Florida's West Coast since 1979, the firm has clients in more than seventy countries throughout the world.

Market Technologies ranked on the Fast Fifty list of Tampa Bay's fastest growing companies for a number of years. In 1999 it ranked as the twenty-ninth fastest growing private company in Florida, and in 2004 was named to the prestigious Inc. 500 magazine list of the 500 fastest growing private companies in the United States out of more than 500,000 companies that competed. Well-known companies that have been selected for the Inc. 500 list of the next generation of world-class companies in the past include Microsoft, Oracle, Morningstar, and E*Trade.

Company Information:

Market Technologies, LLC

E-mail address: forex@tradertech.com

Internet Web site address: www.tradertech.com

Phone:

USA and Canada: 800-732-5407
United Kingdom: 0-800-0186-502
Australia: 1-800-992-327

Others: 813-973-0496

Fax: 813-973-2700

This book, along with other books, is available at discounts that make it realistic to provide it as a gift to your customers, clients, and staff. For more information on these long lasting, cost effective premiums, please call us at (800) 272-2855 or you may email us at sales@traderslibrary.com.